CONVERSATIONS WITH MARY
The Descent into Dementia

CONVERSATIONS WITH MARY

The Descent into Dementia

JENNIFER CLARKE

Books by the author

Thru My Eyes and in My Words
What a Pain!
Thru My Eyes and in My Words Too

Published 2020

Book design by Paper Horse Design & Publishing

ISBN 978-0-9925877-3-4

NATIONAL
LIBRARY
OF AUSTRALIA

A catalogue record for this
book is available from the
National Library of Australia

To Mary,
Thank you for walking part of your journey with me.
I will be forever honoured.

I acknowledge that my creativity is 'powered' by the soul of my faith.

Introduction

I met Sister Mary Magdalene Quinn in early high school, a place I was hell-bent on getting out of without learning much in the way of educational skills. That was, until Mary hit me with a non-lethal projectile (piece of chalk). She was one of my teachers at St Puix X High School in Kempsey, New South Wales. She attempted to teach me Geography and Math. I found her to be a particularly disagreeable teacher but, then again, I was a rather obnoxious student.

My respect for Mary started the day of the chalk-throwing. Not because of her unique attention-getting ways or wicked throwing arm, but because she taught me to listen and to take in what was happening around me. Mary was one of the people who helped start me on the rather bumpy road of self-discovery. For this I will be forever grateful.

As I grew in maturity, so did my friendship with Mary. She became a mentor to me, a wise woman. She was one of the brightest and smartest women I knew.

What was the genesis for this rather unusual project? Love and empathy: Love for Mary and empathy for the journey that she was facing.

I can only describe Mary's behaviour when she started to get an inkling of her condition as frantic. It was as if she was trying to run fast enough that the dementia would not catch up to her. Mary initially had a good dose of denial and anger. Even through the eventual acceptance, there was still some irritation.

A discussion was born out of a comment Mary made back in 2011-12 when she was in what I considered the 'denial stage': she was losing things but was able to come up with plausible answers as to why. She was also *having difficulties finishing a project she was working on. Mary's comment was along the lines of having 'nothing left to give'. To me, she sounded scared and distressed.*

How the thought for this strange project found its way to the surface of my mind, I have no idea, but I am grateful it did. Mary took to the idea with alacrity and we discussed it often. Mary trusted me to share the final moments of her journey on this planet. For me this was, and always will be, a profound honour.

'Conversations with Mary' is not a religious account, per se, but it is discussions with a religious woman. After she quoted 'God is good' to me several times, I couldn't help but liken Mary's journey to that of the biblical character Job-a good and faithful servant on a journey through the loss of family, wealth and health.

Mary joined the Grafton Sisters of Mercy in the early 1950s. Her initial interaction with the Sisters was during her schooling years where she attended school at Cowper on the Lower Clarence. She remained with the Sisters until her death in 2016.

Mary did not believe that God was making her suffer here on earth. Throughout her illness, Mary's faith remained unshaken.

I came to realise that the book was not just about Mary Quinn the person but Mary Magdalene Quinn the woman of Faith. They cannot be separated. Nor could the illness separate them.

Constructing the Chronicle

When we decided to write this book, *we did not think it through very well— how were we going to document the progression? If this had been some kind of professional study, I would have failed miserably. Yes, we discussed that we were going to document Mary's descent into dementia—but not the how and when. The question of when resolved itself as I wrote down a series of her poignant words on the 8th December 2013. It showed both Mary's emotion and the earlier stages of her disintegration.*

Whilst my empathy remained, it was no longer a major motivating factor in continuing the project. I had become fascinated with our conversations and wondered where Mary's mind would take us next.

I soon hit a snag. After spending the 4th April 2014 getting writer's cramp trying to document what was being said, I knew that I was losing parts of the conversation. From that point on I began to tape our conversations.

The next problem was timing and logistics: I lived over four hours away. So I made a commitment to come and see Mary every 4-6 weeks during her final years. Sadly, there were times I was not able to keep to that commitment because of my own health issues.

While the book is called 'Conversations with Mary', to be more factual I could have called it 'Questions for Mary' as most of our discussions were initiated by me asking Mary a question. There were long periods of silence throughout and times where I struggled to wake Mary's mind. Sometimes I didn't know when to shut up; to realise when Mary was thinking, as opposed to having lost the thread of the conversation. As a result, I think I missed some of what she was trying to say. I do wonder where her mind would have taken us if I had not tried to prompt!

Witnessing Mary's frustration at trying to construct a sentence will—I hope—help bring you closer to understanding the pain the dementia caused such a brilliant mind.

Reading this chronicle is an exercise in concentration, a conversational jigsaw, if you will, trying to understand what Mary is attempting to articulate. You may get a different understanding to what I gleaned and at times no one will ever know where Mary's mind was taking her.

I still do not have a logical reason as to why I undertook this project. Fascination and love notwithstanding, it has taken a lot of energy, time and resources; and yet I always felt compelled to continue. Who would be interested in the conversations dredged up from the hallways of Mary's crumbling mind? I may never know but it has been an honour.

I hope this transcription of our meandering conversations will give you some insight and understanding of Mary's final journey here on earth.

Throughout the book, Mary's comments are in regular font, *mine are in italic. Brief descriptions are added in bold (like this). Ellipses (...) are a break in the conversation due to thought or possible confusion.*

At times I did not understand Mary's words. The apparent spelling errors are my attempts to translate her words by spelling them phonetically. The only editing done was to remove names and conversations that I felt were of a private nature.

Mary Magdalene Quinn
29th August 1933 – 9th March 2016

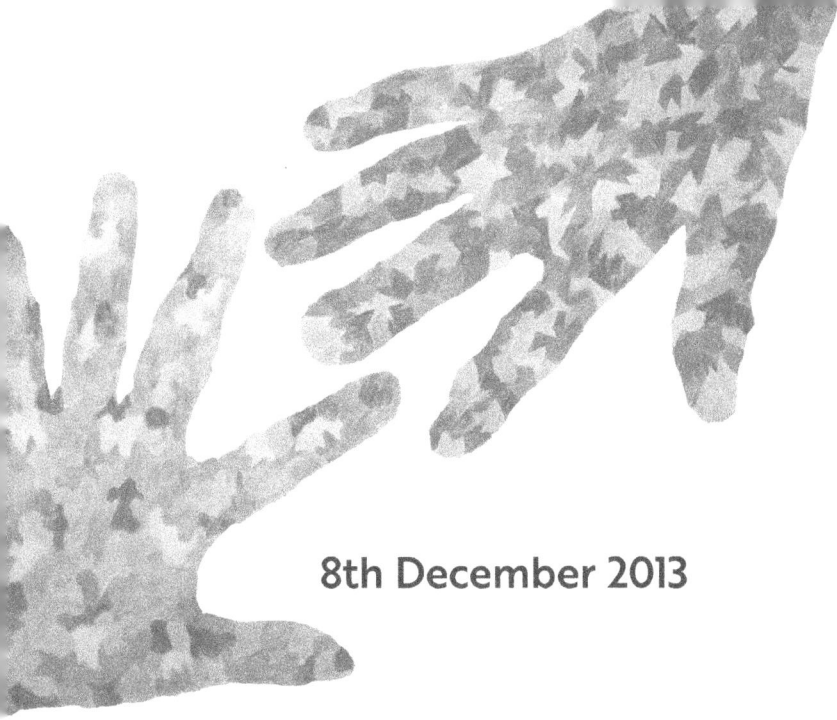

8th December 2013

I'm losing my memory, not my ability to feel pain.

If I've made a choice, please help me to remember that choice.

If this isn't my choice, why am I here?

My memory loss is isolating me.

You can walk away. I cannot!

I still have goals.

Do you even try to understand my struggle?

Why do you think your displays of power won't make me want to bite you!

I feel we are still friends.

4th April 2014

Mary, you just said something to me. I think you said 'I feel like a stranger to myself'. Is that what you said, Mary?
It wasn't exactly.
What do you think you just said?
I think that is what I said. Um! I don't know myself.
Is that painful?
Yes.
Why?
I'm sad. I'm frightened. I must be silly.
No. That is an amazing thing you have said to me. You are not silly. Unwell, yes! It is so hard having this happen. What frightens you the most?
I don't know. I'm frightened that something will go wrong. I don't know what that means. I'm always afraid I'm going the wrong way.
Can I still share this story with other people?
Yes.

Are you feeling agitated at the moment?
Yes very agitated.
Why is that?
Because I was always someone who was right ... not that I mean that I thought I knew everything. I don't. I was ... able to work with things ... especially with

2

things … especially the things in front of me. What am I going to do about this? [Sigh!]

It's frustrating not being able to get it out there.

Yes. This is what I live under sometimes and I have to be able to live with it.

Living with the struggle of not knowing who you are?

Yes.

Is it hard losing you?

Sometimes I am very angry about it.

Do you remember to be angry?

No. No I try to sometimes … in a big way … it's not your business Mary. Your business is this … There are other people walking the same path and they're the ones who have to look after it. I'm going to have to get out of it … I'm going to be OK. It is something I cannot manage at the moment so I'm going to have to try and manage it.

So you are going to try and get others to look after you?

No I don't think I meant that. I think I heard (meant) … yes I supposed I've looked … I think I'm going to have to let it go and go with the flow … something that I have to remember to know. [Sigh!] I'm on a track.

Do you think you are on track now?

No I don't.

A song is coming to mind–'Lose yourself in me and you will find yourself. Lose yourself in me and you will find yourself'.

The talking upsets me.

You'd like a quieter place?

Mmm! Julian of Norwich - 'All shall be well. All shall be well'. You don't have to worry any more. It doesn't mean that you don't have to do it. I get a bit frightened that I am on the wrong track.

Thanks for sharing that with me Mary.

You're welcome.

9th August 2014

Mary is crying.

Is this what it feels like to lose yourself? To not know yourself? Is this what the dementia is like?

I go to another place. We get into the ... I can see ... I cannot tell you. We go up up in the um! ... where am I? Doesn't know herself but God is here in the chapel at St Michaels! I am not unaware.

Do you realise what is going on?

There are people here with me and there are people with me at home but ...

It is a very distressing illness to have Mary.

Yes.

And it really gets to you. I mean to be losing part of yourself every day ... damn cruel!

I'm okay. That's the first real knot I got ...

And sometimes you come across people who do not know what it is like to have dementia and they can make things more stressful for you. They can get frustrated with you and you can feel that.

Yeah!

And that can make you all the more upset and maybe that is what happened this morning.

Well I think that what happened was the experience of the fact that this house doesn't have my clothing in it the way that my sisters in the convent looked after my things. I nearly had a conniption. Have you ever heard of a conniption?

You have conniptions all the time. Didn't you know Mary Quinn is famous for her conniptions?

[Laugh] Well, there you are. You've made me laugh. Why isn't it when you have dementia you cannot remember the good things in life, but you can remember the bastards?

God is good. God is good and he is with me. Is that OK to say?

Yes, Mary and I think that it is a miracle that someone with dementia is able to say that. One of the things that you find really hard is your inability to pray including saying the rosary. You cannot remember the Our Father and the Hail Mary.

OK bad day when I screamed at that lady. I hope that the lady has forgotten what happened.

How could anyone forget you?

[Laugh].

Oh we're cooking with gas girl!

[Laugh].

I... There is something in the air this week that's not here... feeling from now. I feel that there is nothing here, nothing here, nothing here.

Nothing here for what?

For me.

So this is like a strange place?

There is nobody here with it since yesterday. I'm feeling. I've got nothing!

Nothing of who Mary Quinn is? Or nothing as in possessions?

Yes and why aren't you doing something about what is happening to me?

Do you understand what is happening?

Yes, there is a something that happens to some people and it buggers up your life and everything gets knocked about. Anyway, leave it to God. The other thing is I recognise that this place an manage it all. I'm worrying again.

Do you think you would rather be totally demented where you know nothing...

NO! Why?

I'm just asking. Because this is such a struggle. The agitation and you being upset and being anxious. Not being able to remember things. Not knowing yourself...

What would you do instead?

I would think that the person would know nothing.

Well that would be pretty good ... um! No it is not. I don't think I would want to do that. I just want to be here with the people who are here now. It feels quite ... I don't know.

What does it feel like when someone says they are not coming to see you because you've got dementia?

Well it's awful. I keep wondering why. MC ... um is there an MC? I was so happy when somebody had told me that they had seen M. They had talked to her and M had talked to them. I was so glad that she had some knowing.

It is difficult for some people to see how much you've lost. They feel uncomfortable and do not know how to talk to you or what to talk about. The silence for them can be very difficult.

I'm out of it.

What do you mean?

I'm not in it. What's going on here, I'm not in it. I had a dreadful night the night before last, because I couldn't find the way to get to bed.

You don't feel like you're part of life?

Yes. Not my life, this life.

This life is no longer your life!

Yes.

That's an amazing statement.

Your birthday.

I like it that somebody recognises it. This group has no reason to be happy about me.

They feel that because of the dementia, they won't remember that it is your birthday?

No the people here will celebrate, but the people out there won't remember. I am Mary Magdalene Quinn.

And what a beautiful woman you are Mary Magdalene Quinn.

Thank you. My grandmother decided my name. Mary Magdalene at the feet of Jesus has chosen the better path. In my earlier days ...

Those that judge are often looking at themselves when they judge.

It is so true for all of us.

Mary talked at length about her frustration having to get help to get into bed and doing her daily activities. She stated that she felt useless and demeaned.

I know it is easy for me to say you do not need to feel demeaned and useless. Just know that you are worth the help that is being given to you.

Well thank you God for sending you today.

I'm lucky to have a friend like you Mary. It is a precious gift from God, our friendship.

Yes.

Who else can I stir the $#!% out of when I want to!

[Laugh].

I'm also a naughty friend!

[Laugh].

It's about your journey and about how you are coping with losing your mind. Hazel Hawke, she just brought dementia to the forefront of every body's minds.

Why have I done you good?

You arrived at the right time. I had been crying.

What is it like to cry for you?

I probably think it is wrong. It's wrong. It's wrong. Um you are not supposed to do that. You are supposed to be strong.

Didn't you cry very often when you were young?

No. I didn't need to because there was so much love around. My parents and grandmother were amazing people.

So you cried this morning because you did not feel the love around?

I cried this morning because I felt I was nothing. Me, I had lost it.

Mary had disappeared?

Yeah. I know I have plenty of people around who do come to see me.

You remember the statement that you made that you didn't cry because you were surrounded by people that love you?

No, but I might think about it. My mother was not a hitting person but I got one big wack but I have no idea what I did. I cried and cried. Dad said don't get upset about it. You did do the wrong thing we have to teach you not to do things that are not right. I think I replied that nobody loved me. But overall we were very well loved. You said something about dementia and you not knowing them. Why do people get dementia? My worry was that, um, was that I wouldn't know you.

I think that you will always remember that you love me. You might not know who that idiot is in front of you making funny noises, but you will always remember that I am somebody important to you.

[Laugh]. When you left yesterday I do not know what I was thinking that I might not be there when you come.

I made a promise that I would continue to come until you had died.

I am worried that in my dementia I would put you out... that doesn't make sense. [Sigh!] I've got dementia and I've got you as a friend and I love her greatly and she doesn't understand that [Snort!].

You're thinking that your dementia will put me out of your life?

Something like that.

Never! You are not the Mary Quinn that I used to know, but you are still the Mary Quinn that I love.

You have your own life and you are in other lives with other people.

Um! Are you saying that I've got a split personality Mary?

I don't think so. I don't know. I made a life-decision based on the Cowper nuns. I could see that these people were doing a wonderful service. What they did inspired me to become a nun and to live the life I have lived.

So you are saying that what you have achieved in life you are happy with? Is there anything that you still like to do, that you haven't done?

It wouldn't matter now. It is beyond me. I haven't the energy to do it anymore and that's okay. I am glad that there are people who keep me going. The dementia is making trouble in my life. I'd be gone if I didn't have friends. My life at the present time is that I try to remember God. I'm grateful for the things that are in this place and I'm grateful that somebody looks after me. I don't hurt physically. I know what I'd like to do, but I don't know what I'd be able to do but can't do it.

There are a lot of things that you used to be able to do, that you cannot do now. Is that what you are trying to say?

Yes. M. lives across the road and can do what she wants to do. I cannot do that. Somebody has to help me do it. Anyway ... what is is! I don't have the um ... I can't do it.

How does that make you feel?

I cannot do what I'd like now. It's not just ...

1st November 2014

If you don't lose I have a head.
Praise the Lord! So dementia doesn't knock you out of your head?
No!
So what does it do?
Well, I could possibly do more things... I think it was the doctor in Grafton who diagnosed the dementia problem. But I still have a brain! The thing that makes me worst is the noise and carry on. It makes me angry and frustrated. This is it. I am in this issue. It is not going to change.

What have I done for you in your life?
Mary you have helped me to connect to my potential.

When that lady put me in this place... well that just knocked me off the wall.
Do you feel as if you are in God's waiting room?
NO! Something hit me the other day, but I don't have any thought that I am going to die. That's not what I am thinking about now.
So what made you so angry about being put here? Is the anger about your perception of not been given a choice?
That was a very big, big frustrating, angry emotion for me.
If you could get hold of her would you be angry with her?
No I think what she did was wrong. I was being cut off before I knew what I was being cut off about. If I had someone explain to me what was happening

to me... I would not have been knocked over by that.

So it was handled badly?

Yes.

Do you want me to shoot them?

[Laugh!] I'm letting it go. There are other ways of doing this. My memories help keep me awake. I'm glad I like music. It has helped me. I sit here thinking about my past. I also sit here wanting people to engage me.

Is it a privilege to get old?

No. It happens but it doesn't bother me. No... that's not right it um I um can't do what I used to do and I can't even small things I can't do them and that brings in people who look after me. I'm a baby all the time — physically. I need that physical help.

6th December 2014

I think because of my life and my friends and my family I've been given a lot. I look up and see the things in this place and that is beautiful and there are times when I just cry over it [tears].
Because you know what you've lost?
I can't share. I find myself hearing someone say something, a word um I enjoy this sort of thing so in one way I think I'm very blessed.
So you are ignoring your pain?
No it's not pain… um it is pain but I don't think I'm ignoring it I can pass by something a child says and I cry.
Because it reminds you of what you've lost?
[Silence]
And you know that this is what dementia does to you. Is it the frustration?
Yes. But I've come to these two or three things. Its dementia and it is not going to go different. In the beginning I was killing everybody for my doing it… having it. I was thinking this morning if I could have someone with me all the time, if some lovely lady… your coming is fantastic. I can laugh, I can smile and I feel that everyone one of the people who work here and for me, how could I be cranky about them helping me.
Only a saint could say that Mary.
Honestly I am grateful for what you do and the others do. I wish I could get out of here.
Mary Magdalene Quinn are you not human?

[Laugh!]
I'm glad that amuses you sister!
[Laughter]
So you agree with me that you are human?
Oh yes.
Well live with it sister, you are not perfect.
I could kick you.
Feel free. You wouldn't get far because I'd kick you back and then we'd both probably fall over. Mary you are human and being human means that you are not perfect.
That's right. I don't want to be perfect. I just want to be connected with others.
And that is what the dementia is taking away from you? It is taking away from you that connection?
Yes. [Sadness in the voice]
I can see that this is one of the things that make you so frustrated. And as a human being you have that right to be frustrated. That is not wrong. That is your reality and you have a right to say damn it, I do not like this. I do not want it to happen and it is making me angry. You have every right to feel this.
Yes.
Because it is really, really yucky what you are going through. And these women who nurse you and care for you understand that. They understand your frustration.
It is the loss. The loss is very painful. Yes.
And the knowledge that you know that you are going to lose even more is very painful.
Yes. Yes. And I just have to take it.
Frustrating
Well um the only thing about... none of the sisters or my friends have not said nothing about losing it um I in the beginning it knocked me totally, but I at well it's lost. You've got to take it 'cause it will not come back.

Do you remember when you were first told that you were suffering from dementia?
I was very angry because the person who told me... I wasn't told I thought it was done very badly. I was put onto the nursing home when I was diagnosed.
What are you talking about? Why can't you just say what it is?
They were scared to tell you what was wrong?
Poor things!

I knew that you had dementia because of your symptoms.

I didn't know it - that I had dementia. I just couldn't work out what people were saying.

Most people get an inkling that something is going on.

Well I really had no idea that I was becoming forgetful and um I find it interesting that I can still get something back out of my mind. The fact that it wasn't discussed with me…do you realise etc., I don't remember anybody saying to me that I am losing it. I was angry that she didn't tell me anything…I wasn't told! Whatever the way it was done or not it's not going to change the situation that I am in. I don't think anyone really told me that it was a problem.

12th December 2014

This was never meant to happen Mary.
Yes it was meant to happen. Everything is meant to happen if it happens.

We talked about a Christmas ornament – a snow cone that Mum owned that I gave to Mary. I had to explain it three times. Eventually I said:

Is your dementia playing up?
No, you just haven't explained it well enough!
[Laughter]
I would like people who I know me around me.
Are you feeling lonely?
No I do not feel lonely at all. Lonely for me is um what would I be lonely about? I don't think I get lonely um. I would like to talk to them and stay awake. I want to talk to people who know me.

15th January 2015

It's an awful thing and on the other side it's not so much. Sometimes I've had nice conversations with the girls here and I've try to be able to help some of the ones that wouldn't have the head to know what was going on and there is one lady here who is a beautiful old woman like me and she has three boys and two are married and she lives across the road and she didn't catch on that she wasn't at home and up to now and now it has hit her that she is here. Emotionally she was upset. I could cry for her.
Could you cry for yourself?
I think I have sometime but when I got to the edge um when I didn't know and I was angry that I was told... I was angry with the way I was told that this was what was wrong and it nearly killed me. It took me quite a time to believe that there was something wrong in me and wasn't able to be fixed. But I feel I've got to be happy here. Yeah!

So what are you thinking now?
How did they pick it up that there was something wrong with me? The dementia! Have I changed?
Usually they pick it up through symptoms. Like the things that you have done - like you kept on losing your wallet; you kept on repeating yourself; same stories; asking the same questions.
They can also do scans of your head to see if something shows up. For someone sitting on the outside watching someone 'lose their mind' it's

really hard to watch that ... people struggling with sentences or memories. They are not themselves anymore. Even though you are still Mary to me um you are not the Mary that I grew up with, you are not the Mary I knew when I was in the convent. You have a completely different personality now. You couldn't throw chalk to save yourself.

[Laughter]

But in another sense you are still Mary. You are Mary and you have the soul of Mary. So, what do you think about what I just said?

Well I think that what you say that Mary, me, is still here for some parts anyway ... [confused babble] ... being able to talk has and is important to me. You know when I hear some of those people out there who do not have a clue who they are or where they are [other patients].

Does it worry you that you are going to be like them in the end?

If it is going to be, it has to be.

So you are accepting of that?

Yes. I'm not going to waste energy on what isn't going to be fixed.

To be so accepting of the fact that one day you may not know anything. Wow!

Well I'm hoping that it's not true.

[Laughter]

Fair enough. My personal opinion is the cruelty of the slowness of dementia is really yuck, really inhumane. I suppose it's the word I am looking for because once someone knows that they have got dementia, it would be good if it could happen straight away so that they do not have to suffer through the loss of their dementia. You know how you were diagnosed with dementia so many years ago ...

Yeah!

... and it's been a gradual decline for you. Has that been hard for your or have you not noticed the gradual decline in your abilities?

Well ... I think because I had to take it I can um when something goes wrong I am able to deal with it in some way. See for example if one of the things that um spoken about several times the not remembering and the not being able a lot of that I've worked at through if this is it I'll have to see if I can manage what I can and can't do. I mean the fact that you and I can talk to each other is important.

Do any of the other visitors talk to you like this?

Ah no um there is a um actually I had a whole run this year just finished a number of people I've taught and people I've worked with in that area I don't care and God is God and I think I've come to somewhere around to I can be in control oh woe is me! I do not think that they pity me I think I've done okay. I don't think I've talked to anybody about the dementia recently. They treat me as they've treated me before. I know that I can have a good conversation with them.

Do any of the people who visit you treat you like a child?
NO!

So they've treated you with respect?
Yes. I haven't had many people um it's not them. I can't get at something like one of the M's and see if I can get some singing lessons. That didn't bother me when you said that she wouldn't be able to … There is people for me to talk to now the H's are people I can talk to.

It takes a lot of courage to get old.
R is a lovely lady. My first of the family P had was great, she lives in Ulmarra. You know where there is where they made P and all the sisters I've got. T came for half a day all of that is going on all the time. T hubby has dementia. That doesn't bother me

This is a very distressing part of the dementia—knowing that you've got it and trying to cover it up.—talking about M. You were a bit like that at the beginning.
I just thought it was something but I couldn't work out what it was.

Yeah the brain stops working properly. The mathematical equations go in one ear and out the other, then fly off never to be grabbed and brought back again. One of the things I've been noticing is a lot of highly intelligent people—you're the most intelligent woman I've met in my life—have been tending to get dementia. All I can say is thank God I am not all that bright.
[Laughter]

From the moment I met you I knew that you were one of the most intelligent woman I knew and that was one of the things that I really admired. Here was this woman who was a brilliant mathematician walking through life so confident in her abilities. You were a confident woman and that was one of the things that I admired about you.
And now I've lost it!

You haven't lost my respect or love.
No. No. No.

You've lost the ability to engage that part of your brain, that's part of the woman that you've lost. You haven't lost your soul or your spirit.
NO. NO.

You haven't lost the important things that are part of you. Can you understand what I am saying?

I can yes.

Do you agree that you've lost the ability to engage that part of your brain?

Oh yes. I um somebody piece of info on paper I pick it up and put in in the bin.

Because you cannot read it?

I can't read or write.

What is that like not to be able to read or write any more? What does that feel like?

Well it's I've lost my ability to do something when I made the decision to do this singing I thought it might not work I know that that's been dropped and it because I've given it up I've given it up. I'm not like I was when I realise what this was like. I was sad that I lost my abilities and it is hard that I cannot things that everybody gets like I'd like to oh get stutter ... I'm lost.

In what sense are you lost?

I know that I am still me and I'm sorry sad that I cannot do things get things whatever but if what will be, it will be.

You are a courageous lady Mary Quinn!

I've got God!

And that is why I am so lucky to have you as a friend. You still inspire me ... you will always inspire me. Isn't it great to be mates!

It is ... I noticed that ah in me probably just the last couple of months I'm find myself if I'm singing something I cry. I don't cry it just comes up.

Jesus is for me personally someone who is an example of what it is to be good and faithful and honest. JC is the way to God. It is the path you follow. Jesus says that his way to God is to live a life of Mercy and you definitely live a life of Mercy.

You know it is very hard there is nobody to say something about I'm wondering a bit if I'm going to lose get away from me, however I know God is good.

Why?

I just know.

And that is faith.

God is good.

You are an inspiration

I'd like to you know to have a chat with someone who knows about faith. I haven't been to Holy Communion for two and a bit years. I've sometimes got it.

Do you think that is true or do you think your memory might have been muddled?

No. No. I think I really it's too big and I'd say back to God it is up to you please. Anyway I haven't been um ...

Have I made you sad Mary?

No, no um um there is a girl that this lady who the lady one of the nuns who finished it off to work and not work.

Um, she retired?

Yes she retired, anyway she gave to a young woman something to um for me to talk to her and I'm hoping that I'll get something out of that in the line of ...

Does it have to be a priest that you wish to talk to?

No.

What about F? I could ask her to come and talk to you.

Yeah thank you um I don't think I could ... I'd really like to get that thing song I want to get someone behind me to help me.

16th January 2015

So why do you think the dementia sent you off last night?
I refuse to do things.
What kind of things?
We were going to um I um...
You look as cranky as a cut snake. You feel cranky?
No I'm not now.
So why were you cranky last night?
I was going to have them all killed.
You were going to have them all killed! Wow! That's very un-Christian of you Sister Mary.
Yes.
So you were violently angry during the night?
Really the thing was, I was worried. I was worried I uh...
And no one would listen to you?
Yeah.
You felt frustrated?
YES!
And that made you angry because you couldn't get anyone to understand you.
Yes. And I was frightened that I had done something like...
You made the staff upset and that upset you?
Mary nodded.

Anyway let's get on another thing. I've been waiting for it.
What would you like to talk about?
I've been waiting for you to talk.
You can think of it in your head but you cannot get it on the tongue?
Yeah … um this is nice [Mary was eating some KFC].

This is really beautiful [looking at a plant].
Some people are really good with planting and gardening. I myself have a black thumb. My plants have a tendency to keel over and die.
[Laugh]
Are you frustrated now?
No. I would like to spend some time up the hill.
Pardon?
Where you went today.
The Carmelites?
Yeah.
That would be nice. When was the last time that you went on retreat? Can you remember?
No. I have namentia!
You have namentia? You mean dementia?
[Laughter]

Aren't people funny?
Worse than funny.
In what way?
Um they want everything.
So you think people are greedy?
Yes greedy.
Do you think that what is half the problem today is that people are greedy?
They are certainly not nice. But there is also the wonderful people.
Like the one that I am sitting in front of!
Serious?
Serious!

So what frustrated you so much this morning that you had to throw your breakfast across the floor?
Well I don't know. It's frightened me and it's been done a couple of times. When I got up there was noise around and in it there was a were ah people and then while I was lying on my bed after having been woken up I heard

21

this Mary (other Mary) when she gets wanting to know you can hear her she was making little noise and she was saying saying saying and I got up in the finish and that was what I thought there is a way that you can put people off it was awful if she didn't get out of it she would get killed.

I'm not sure I understand that Mary. You were worried about this other Mary getting killed?

Yes.

So, why did you throw your breakfast for then?

Well I was trying to do something that Mary wouldn't.

You were trying to protect Mary by throwing your breakfast?

No She was the one was in trouble. I was just so mad!

What were you mad at?

Mary was in trouble.

You were worried for her. You got angry?

Sigh! No. Oh No I thought I was what and I wanted to I was all mad.

I think you are all confused.

That's right. That's right. Dementia.

Do you think you've got dementia?

I wanted to get somewhere but I couldn't pick it up.

Okay so you threw the breakfast hoping that someone would notice?

And help me.

Help you because you were so angry?

Yes.

Do you think they would have got angry at you for throwing the breakfast? Would they have helped you?

I don't know.

But you're feeling better now?

I am.

Well I'm totally confused!

[Laughter]

I got locked in the bathroom.

Pardon?

Um ...

You cannot remember. That is the thing about dementia. Your short term memory seems to be pretty spotty. But you are still my Mary.

I don't know what it is.

What happened last night?

It just upsets me. I'm terrified of it.

22

Do you see it as part of your dementia?
[Silence]
You're terrified that it is going to happen all the time and that you are going to lose control of yourself?
[Nod] I have very few people around me.
You've said that a lot. Are you lost or are you lonely or are you both?
I'm not lonely. I can sit with myself but it's getting more that sitting with myself.
Have you sat with yourself and suddenly realised that hours have passed without noticing?
No.
So what do you do when you sit with yourself?
That is an interesting question. I think if I um there is nothing else to say or is God or the future I think would be what I think about.
You think about God and your future. Is that what you are saying?
No I know when I ah am talking in or for or whatever God I'm doing git just myself and then I would go but the other way if I was is go is what's the future but it is not very long. It's not something that I get very caught up in but I don't get unhappy for example I have my sisters my family I don't I think of God when I think of those that love me. I think what I'm thinking ... [Laugh] I sometimes don't know what I'm doing without worrying about thinking um but I think more now . . .

We were interrupted by the nurse.

Twice I've done that and I can't get I'm frightened of it happening again. This morning was dreadful. But then I was thinking this morning that this is what I've got.
We could give you a nickname—mucked up Mary.
[Laughter]
What are you thinking?
About last night and what was happening and why it was happening. I'm frightened of um falling over.
It hurts, especially when you hit the ground.
Well I have hit the ground. When I came here I had five hits on the ground and then I got better for a while but I think it is happening again. I don't know ...
It's okay to not know.
Yeah. I'm glad you found me.
I think God found us both. Our friendship was always meant to happen Mary. There was some kind of connection when you were the teacher and I

was the child. People would sometimes ask me why I keep coming up here when you have dementia and I say: Mary might have dementia but she is still my friend and that you are a woman who has done so much for me.

Keep on keeping please.

Always. And sometimes it is good just to sit in silence and enjoy each other's company.

Yes.

We do not have to talk all the time.

No.

28th February 2015

If I am upset or cranky she helps bring me down.
She brings you back to calmness?
Yes.
So, what makes you cranky and upset?
Um! I did a dreadful thing the other night. A lady about my age...
102!
[Laughter]
...anyway something happened she is a nurse and she said something...
And you got angry?
That's not nice. I'm usually a nice person.
There is nothing wrong with losing your temper, even if you are a nice person. Would you consider me a nice person?
Um yes.
I lose my temper and I fantasize about hitting people but I don't though. Sometimes I've lost my temper and have yelled at people. I've even been known to call others names occasionally. I called Mum an old cow once. You know what she did... she mooed at me.
[Laughter]
We get cranky Mary and you are very frustrated with your illness. Tell me, what do you think of Euthanasia?
I think I would go to the edge and um um not have people who have been been nothing nothing that is so I um there's a little lady here what's her

name ... [unintelligible mumble].

We are talking about Euthanasia.

Yes yes I am coming to that ... she went to the edge of the world ...

What do you mean by the edge of the world Mary?

I don't know.

I asked you what you thought of euthanasia and for a very brief period you sparked up. You brain started firing and you said some words that were very clear and then you went back to being confused.

Does Mary Quinn have the right to say that 'when I get to a certain point I wish to die'? Do you think you should have that right or do you think that it is in God's hands and leave it there.

Um I don't like the matter of people being so so sick and really over the edge ...

So people have the right to end their lives?

Well I don't think I'd say that. I think I would leave it to God.

We are going to disagree on this one.

The thing that I would look at ... I have not looked at this much I'm using this lady as what happens. It is just so much if at this time I was going out of the world um I would prefer that you would say it, get out of it quick. If you know that I'm not happening ... heavens heaven ... I don't think God would be doing that!

But he also doesn't like to see people suffer. Are you also saying this?

Yeah.

Do you think that if God gave us the ability to end a person's suffering we shouldn't use it?

Yes!

Then again we have the ability to kill each other - through free will. I do not think God would be very happy with us using our free will for this.

It's not for me.

Why did you say it is not for me?

No! [Said loudly]

You are interested?

Yes but you can't get it ... in here ... [Mary points to her head].

You mean it goes in one ear and out the other?

I hear little things and um there interesting things um um but the it's not something that I go into I heard something recently about woman ...

Does it frustrate you when you hear things and then you lose it?

No it doesn't frustrate me at all. I haven't got and because of that and because of the dementia ... I think this is one of my um ... beliefs and this is a very big one for me God is good. You would never get me not to believe that. God is good.

What does that mean for you?

It's a it's a bit like a out in the world somewhere and I am gonna do something awful. It doesn't matter. God is good and sometimes when people are talking about things awful people bits of anger God is good.

It doesn't matter what happens with your life, God is still good!

Yes.

Even when you have dementia and you've lost your ability to think, to pray, to read and write; God is still good?

Yes and I've in the beginning I didn't think God had anything to do with it. Might have said a few prayers now and again and it's there and God is good. And I've come a long way.

You are an amazing woman Mary Quinn and you have a beautiful smile.

Have I got blue on my eye?

Your eyes are blue, yes.

That's Irish.

Would you like to go and live in Ireland?

Not to live but I think it is something that I inherited from Dad. When Mum died Dad said "I should have known. She always wants to get it first." [A belly laugh from Mary] Mum was pretty pushy but she was a lovely lady. They were both very loving people. I cannot remember Dad getting cranky. Mum ran the home.

Did your dad ever get back to Ireland?

The dementia doesn't bother me now I think.

You were still quite functional until about 18 months ago.

Yeah. When I was early when I came out ... how long have I been here?

You've been here 18 months in this facility.

18 months?

Probably early 2013 you were not functioning very well. Meaning you've not been able to care for yourself for about two years now.

Oh! All right. I don't think I've ever looked after myself.

What do you mean?

There has always been someone there to help me.

You mean you have never been able to shower yourself?

I don't like ... um I'm a bit off on that one.

Yeah you're a bit confused girl.

Yeah.

[Laughter]

You've not always been this dysfunctional Mary. Do you remember that?

Yes. Yes. I appreciate what other people do for me. I was um … when I um got I got the stuff um I had um I we lived in together um I never had to have someone I can't do that I'll have to ask someone to do that.

We all need help sometimes. I think maybe you are talking about living in community.

Yes.

Have you ever lived alone in your life ever?

On my own. No. This thing of when the dementia came and I didn't place immediately it's not only living on your own but being on your own in dementia. There's very much a difference.

So what you're saying is dementia makes for a very lonely lifestyle?

Yes and when I said to this lady um! I don't like to say that I don't like it … I've never been spoken to the way I've been spoken to by the head person here. I get what I get from the people who … they are not let that go … for example I have tried to be able to get contact with um people who before dementia I had. Not able to go to the whatever go to where the not.

There is no communicating?

No. Not so long ago people wouldn't …

Are you finding that people are not communicating with you because you have dementia?

I don't think they do anything with me.

That must be frustrating!

Yes. I had there are some things that I have worked out for myself and that's good. I'm glad that my two sisters visited me and told me what the others were up too.

Do you realise that you are that lonely or does it hit you every so often that you are lonely?

I'm not feeling lonely! There is enough in me with God is good.

That is a very strengthening thing for you?

I got to a place at one stage …

So if you are not feeling lonely and people are not communicating with you then what are you feeling?

I'm a good person.

I know you are a good person.

Well I suppose my time and having that way of life having God being always there and also these people and the visitors are enough for me. The fact that I knew and when I had that I went off and had the … lots of people have been wonderful with me. I have some capacity that if I was in somewhere with others that I could communicate with them. I wouldn't stay in my room. I think that convent living was good for me because I liked them I liked what happened. The people were good to me.

The culture was positive for you?

Yes. And I think that at the end I because I um people gave me good people have been nice to me and that has helped me…you've done your bit be grateful.

I don't think it is just dementia. Growing old tends to isolate people.

Oh yeah!

Isolate you from family and friends because you gradually lose the independence that you had as a younger person. Your friends and family are possibly going through the same things and becoming isolated also.

Oh yes.

Age can be cruel mistress!

Yes. Yes.

And we go to our God in various ways. God might be good, but she also has a sense of humour.

[Laughter]

I find our friendship a bit of a miracle don't you?

Well I just take it for granted.

29th February 2015

What do you feel when you get angry?
I shouldn't be doing it.
Why?
Because it is not right.
Do you yell at them or do you try to hit them?
No. No. No. No.
Do you think that they might understand that you are frustrated?
[Mary shakes her head]
You don't think they'd understand?
They don't know that.
I think I understand that you get frustrated because of the way you are and the dementia. You don't think the nurses would understand?
Yes they do! But some others don't.
Does it matter?
Well I don't want to be like that!
Don't you think that it is part of your dementia though?
Umm...
Do you think you are a bad person because you get angry at other people?
No. I don't like being a person who doesn't say nice things to people. Anyway...
I thought you were gonna say you don't like people who were crazy

old coots.
Is that what I am?
Nope. I might be one, but you are not.
I don't think you would be crazy about anything.
I lose my temper too Mary.
Do you?
Oh yeah!
When you are in pain…
Are you in a lot of pain?
Um this leg is pain. [Mary points to her left leg]. But not pain like your pain.
Do you have pain all the time with that leg?
No only when it moves me.

Two days ago my sisters D and P came over to see me and it was just lovely.
What did they talk about?
Everything that the others are doing.
They caught you up on all of the news?
They took me to a place that is okay. I know where they are and what they are doing.
How many sisters have you got Mary?
There were eight sisters and one died.
How old was she?
Not old at all. She had married and lost children and then lost her life with cancer. She was the oldest in the group. There was Ilene, me, D…

Mary spoke with confidence and clarity for twenty-odd minutes about Ilene and her children. I did not need to prompt nor ask questions.

Well I feel better.
In what sense?
I didn't have any breakfast this morning. I couldn't do it because of that woman.
Why? Does she makes you feel cranky.
She doesn't make me feel cranky she um I want her to be out.
And she isn't?
It would be nice but she cannot get her husband back.
You know it would be hard to have lived with someone for many years and then to have suddenly lost them.

Going back to Ilene I thought the best thing that he did, he died from cancer too and Ilene didn't have to do a thing. He set up everything so that she did

not have to worry.
How long ago was this Mary?
How old am I now?
102.
[Loud laughter]
I don't know how old I am.
I think you are in the mid-eighties.
That's right. That's right. Well Ilene would be 80, 80. Um! I think she would be 90. So that fits where I put Ilene.

Silence for about 10 minutes.

Riveting conversation!
Yeees.
[Laughter]
I'm thinking of ... I think I would be only one of the nuns who is um who is not um living on her own.
What makes you say that?
I know that ...
You mean all the rest are living on their own?
Yep.
Why do you say that?

M.B. picked up that you were not wearing your Mercy cross. Have you lost your cross?
No I don't think so.
I could have a snooze now.
I'm feeling a little tired myself but they are going to put food down my neck.
[Laugh]
You mean shovel it in? You don't have to eat if you don't wish too.
I know that. [Sigh!] What did that say?

28th March 2015

Mary was taken on a bus trip to Grafton.

Doughty's organised a beautiful lunch for us. I had fish and it was the most beautiful fish I've ever had.
So you do not have any problems with your food? You can taste really well?
Yes. We came back over here and what I like is that I can remember going, the road and coming back and seeing the things on the road that I've seen before [Mary was very excited explaining all of this]. I am not dead yet! [Laughter] The 'demuncher' didn't take it away... um dementia! [Laughter]
The dementia is demunching you away!
[Laughter] It will just keep on will it?
The dementia?
Yeah.
You don't remember a lot.
I'll be too old!
No Mary it is the dementia.
Hum!
How does that make you feel?
A wobbly yeah. I don't um I think I satisfied myself with what I have. Um I won't run away before I've had enough um ah...
You've lost me there Mary.
The de dementia which has started it goes on on on on on on on on on on...
For the rest of your life.

33

Well I don't worry about that. I have a head and I know this is a bad time and know this is going to be that and I did hear what was wrong and I put it in my pocket and that is where it is now.
You've put it in your pocket!

The next thing, I think it was before um trip, um I told you It was also we went to what was he we went to the pub… I've had two people I love that have gone to God. Mary who I used to hold her hand. She is the mother of the two boys…

Have you got dementia? [Mary asked this while I was sitting making some comments into the recorder]
I'm making conversations for the book we are writing together. Do you remember the book we are doing?
I do.

Were you one of the nuns who became a sister and then went away?
I was the woman who entered the convent with my motorbike.
You are not the only one.
Who else entered with a motorbike?
No this one entered with her husband.
With her husband?
Um!
How can you enter the convent with a husband?
She left the convent and got married and she was you know the lady who did the beautiful ah ah um her sister was a wonderful painting person.
Um! Are you trying to remember who I am?
No! Trying to I know who the lady was who was the painter but I never really got into what her name was but she left went home got married and then he died and she doesn't like Mary Quinn.
And she doesn't like Mary Quinn? Well she is a woman without taste.
[Laughter]
Anyway she is here.

Your eyes are staring off into the distance. Can you see what is happening in Ireland at the moment?
Yes.
You are actually visualising it?
Yes.
How does that make you feel—relaxed, comfortable, happy?

I feel it in my heart.

So your feelings are strong?

Yeah. My Irish feelings are very strong where the waters run in and there is a song about it which is often on the radio. I didn't realise that maybe six from here to McLean that I have Irish eyes. I didn't know that. Someone very recently told me I um have um I have a nice face. Is that right?

You've got a beautiful face Mary and lovely eyes.

I feel sorry for her.

So what are you going to do?

Do you feel that life is passing you by Mary?

No. No I've had a lovely life. I lost my parents. That was the biggest thing for me. I was sitting somewhere and thinking to myself I said oh dear. I'm not very... [confused rambling] ...

I think I've had enough.

You cannot talk?

Hum! We have a thing on the... I can't work it out. Important people for us in Catholic. You have Jesus, Mary all the names you know and the apostles.

Who was Mary's husband?

[Silence]

No, I can't get it. That is one thing the names twist.

You forget them?

But I put this list in my mind and said to myself oh golly I hope that I put dad in that and then I said Dad was dead so he wasn't there. I don't know why I'm talking about this so I better shut up. [Laughter]

You don't know what you're talking about so you better shut up. It'd be nice if we all followed your lead 'cause half of us don't know what we are talking about.

[Laughter]

One thing about me in um a place where there was no real noise. In the room...

You want a quiet room where you can cut out the noise?

Yes.

Before you had dementia do you remember being irritated by noise because I know that every time I come here it is something that you always talk about—the noise in the place?

That wasn't...

Well it is something I observed that noise really irritates you now. I know that it irritates me, but with you it makes you cranky and restless.

Um. What it does to me is that I think some of the people know they are there and they take it. Anyway. What is done is done. Do I make noises with you?

No you are a very gentle lady.

Thank you.

I love you Mary.

I love you.

Even if you don't know my name!

I do know your name I just have to stop every time to work it out um there you are I told you.

If I said my name was Jill would you believe me?

No.

It's Kay.

It's not.

Robyn.

No. I know it and I'll find it.

Georgina.

Nooo!

Marcia.

Na.

Beryl.

No.

Jennifer.

Um Jen Jenny. [Laughter]

You know what it isn't!

Yes.

Isn't it interesting. You can't get it out there … fascinating. The brain is an amazingly mysterious part of our anatomy.

Yes. I thought um the dementia doesn't get into the brain.

Well what do you think it is if it doesn't get into the brain? If you cannot read any more and if can't write any more, if you cannot pray any more …

Yes!

And if you feel that your intelligence is gone what is being affected if it is not the brain?

That's right.

So the brain is not working well which is very frustrating for you. I can remember when I was here last month, one of the things that we talked about was the fact that you find it very disturbing that you cannot pray anymore because you do not remember the prayers and you don't know if you are praying or not but one thing you said was that God was good. You were very strong on that–God is good. No matter how much you have suffered Mary, not matter how much you have gone through, for you God is still good.

I think the early part of my life with dementia was that nobody, I'm not talking about you, that is why you have been so wonderful to me because you told me and I could understand some of what was happening and that it would go on happening but from the powers that be I got nothing about that.

Maybe it is because they didn't know how to say it. A lot of people do not know how to deal with someone who has dementia Mary. Which is really sad as it makes it all the more hard for the person suffering from dementia.

Yeah.

It is a very frightening thing to have.

Yeah.

Have you felt frightened with the dementia?

No no because what the biggest thing for me that I know is I will die and God will be there. I find myself sometimes saying well I'm in a mess and I can say I've just got to sit here and will be done.

God's will be done?

Yes. I've sat in places where I've had to do something and I couldn't do it then and I've thought oh God this is not going to work and well sit here and it will work out. There are some nice ladies here who talk to me about my dementia.

So you would rather people be honest about your illness?

Yes!

And approach it and talk about it.

Yes. And there are things that I get are good. I'm sad about the fact that I can't um it's it hurts that I can't do some things like not being able to read and write and say things and I can't get to people.

Do you mean that you cannot visit them because of your dementia?

Yeah. And I don't know why they don't visit me but I have to take that on.

Is it because that you may have forgotten that they have visited you?

Probably. Somebody um I don't tell me they've seen someone I have not seen they have any way you are here today and that's good.

Do you get embarrassed at any stage that you've lost so much of your memory and can't actually speak about things?

No it's probably like that you know it's there and it is going to happen. I've come to the space where there are beautiful people and I'm not going to get them everywhere but um some people um are not worried think I cannot do

it don't know don't do it. I think my sister who is the first one I think she might have a bit of horror with me not the dementia I don't think she understands what it is. There are people moving on from me...
You are in their past?
Yeah.
How does it feel being in their past?
I feel it's funny sad ... [Silence].

One of these girls I think she to the getting married level and I it's hard for me to know she she um I went to meet her she and her sister are close and one of them said to me 'I love you'...[Mary became emotional then said that she hasn't seen her since]
So there are some things that make you cry and make you regret?
I don't think there is anything that makes me regret. Where do you think that came from?
Well when you cried about not seeing her again, I thought that you might have been having feelings of regret.
No no um it wasn't me that there was a lot of trouble in that.
The family ... you helped her a lot didn't you?
Yes.

Why do you ask am I boring you?
You put a lot of energy into me I just wanted to um make you see that you do.
No you don't bore me, never have bored me and never will bore me.
Yeah.
Cause I really enjoy your company That's why I ask you lots of different questions to help wake you up and make you think about life.
Yeah. Yeah.
Sometimes I am really tired.
Um.
Like yesterday was a hard trip for me and I was in some pain and I'm still in discomfort today. So sometimes it is hard for me to travel. I push myself. This place here where am I?
St Michaels.
I get mixed up between St Michaels and Grafton. Say a little prayer. I want you to pray for something um I've got a thought in my head that um I could get very out of where I am in my um area where I am...
St Michaels.
St Michaels and not be where I am now but to be in the area with MK. The

same place anyway I don't know how I can work what I want or how I want well what am I trying to do um but ... [Confused garble]
What's wrong with ya? You suffering from dementia?
[Laughter] I think I am!

D. is suffering from dementia. It is sad.
Why is what's happening to her sad when you are suffering from the same thing and it is not sad for you?
[Shrug]
Well I'm a person who takes a job and the way I take it is that's it.
What is is?
Yes and the better thing is God.
God is good!
Yes. I am unhappy that I have come into this dreadful condition. Does this make any sense?
Oh yeah!
[Laughter]
That is very okay to feel that way.
Yes. I have you. If you ran away or had something terrible happen to you I would be upset. Here is me Lord telling you ... I'm suffering ...

Why did you leave? Because you were irreligious?
No there were two reasons. I didn't like the idea of someone else making decisions for me.
Yeah.
I found that it was really hard for me in that what I needed to grow as a person was to be able to make decisions about my own life and what way I went in life. That couldn't happen in religious life. And the other reason was–nobody liked my jokes!
[Laughter]
Oh sorry that just came out. See I told you I was irreligious.
You are not irreligious!
The other real reason was that I thought I could serve the Lord better outside of religious life. I um think there would have been something missing in me if I had stayed in religious life. Who I am as a person did not translate well being in religious life. I mean you look at me now, I'm a real country bumpkin. I'm in trousers and cut off sleeves of a flanny shirt. Not real feminine!
I'm a woman!
I'm a very different woman and I'm gay and I can serve the Lord in the gay

community. How are all your friends going?

They are all going well. I serve the Lord in that community. They know that I go to church. They know that I am a spiritual woman and that I pray a lot and I truly believe that God is there and I feel that I can share just by being myself what it is like having the Lord in the world. Obviously I could not have done this in religious life. Ironically it was in religious life that I discovered that I was possibly gay. It doesn't stop me being a Christian. It doesn't stop me being spiritual and it doesn't stop me from being there for people in need and I can do that best outside of religious life.

[Silence]

So why are you still within religious life?

Me?

Yes.

I was thinking about this not so long ago I don't know whether um making and understanding myself but why did I um become a nun and stay one. I'm still at it is I wanted to give. I think I got it from my mother. She was a lady who would give give give. And I think I was one of those myself. The thing that I most want to do is to give.

What do you mean by you want to give?

Um! That is a hard question.

You know why I became interested in religious life Mary? Because you threw a piece of chalk at me in class.

[Loud laughter]

That is not a joke. It is very serious. You threw a piece of chalk at me and by doing that you spoke to me in my language in that you spoke to me as a tough sister. You spoke as someone who I could understand. That is when I first became interested in religious life. Isn't that an amazing thing! You never ever knew. I have joked about that piece of chalk in the past but you and the Lord spoke to me the moment that chalk hit me I thought wow that woman has got something to say. You gained the respect and attention of Jennifer Clarke that day. You were on my wavelength. I think that our friendship was always meant to be.

Anyway you remained a Sister of Mercy because ...

There was something that um when I saw the sister when they were praying people that was part of it another was helping people women really see it was the end of the second world war and people were worried about husbands coming home, have enough money for the children and that part of it was what put me to it. Um I don't know if I told you this um we were side by side two Irish homes Quinn's and Shorts and one of the boys had his

40

eye on me and I liked him a lot but when I was working with going into the sisters. I ran into him a few times but decided to go with the sisters. If I hadn't I might have gone with him but I went with sisters and became a nun and one day this is very important to me. I was quite young. I might have been six or seven. A lot of time and in that place um the kids the boys would go out to the bushes away from town he was great with horses and one afternoon I was on my way home and he brought this beautiful horse. I though he was coming to give it to me. He was bringing it to show it to me and that was the end of our time.

Many years later I went on with the sisters going around [visitation] yeah in the hospital and I went into the hospital and I heard his name. I went in and said hello to him and I could see myself standing in the hospital and I had a talk with him. He was very ill. They couldn't work out what was wrong with him. So when I was leaving I said goodbye to him and said I would see you in the morning. And in the morning he was in heaven. That was very strong in my memory.

Why Mary? Because you felt that you might have been a good wife to him?
No, no, no. I was very strongly a Sister of Mercy. That Mercy bit — Mercy. And the children, I was very strong on kids being cared for. I don't know why I went into that for you but there it is.

I asked the question.
It was more for the children I think then their parents. I was very strong on the kids being able to that was something I was able to get children better placed.

But even though you felt you would serve the Lord by being a giving person what was in it for you personally. Not for the children not for Mercy but for you to be a Sister of Mercy?
When I saw the nuns in Cowper what they were doing I think my there was something about my soul and my connection with our Lady that I was connected too. I um wasn't made for for um having children... [Silence]

What are you thinking?
Why did I um think of marriage. I don't think it ever came into my head.

Because you were so strongly a Sister of Mercy?
Yeah and I the first Christmas I was they were children in need, more than teaching. Did I think I might have told you this one of the kids I had in was um wait a minute now I forget his name...

29th March 2015

Have you ever tried to read anything on paper recently?
No I've put it away.
You've given up reading?
Yes. But I look at the scenery at the hills out there. [Mary points out the window]
There are no hills out there Mary. Just fences and trees.
Yes but they go that way.
So you are not reading because you cannot see or because you cannot comprehend it?
No I can't see it. I think what I've done is said blow the lot.
Because you cannot see?
Because I can't anything that I used too!
Is that frustrating?
Yes it is frustrating. Very.
Do you wanna throw a piece of chalk at me?
[Laughter]

I can see you. Mostly things in this room. I don't know what that is?
That's a lily plant.

You look delightful today. I love that skirt.
[Laugh]

I also like the shirt. It is beautiful.
That's right.

The lady in charge who looks after us. Her name is also your name. Have I told you about her before?
You've talked about a Jenny.
I want to tell her a few things.
About?
About how I am in here and things…
And how are you in here?
A lot better than I…I would like to have a conversation with someone who could have a conversation with me. Someone to come along and say Mary we know you've got dementia come to our place for a while and we'll look after you. Oh I miss that person, I miss that person. So its things like that, that are real, are good things for me in this particular issue.
So you would like to see some of the sisters take you into their home for a little while and care for you?
No it is not that.
Can you explain to me what you were trying to say?
Um there are people who got something in here (pointed to chest) who I actually um there are people who are out there, not in my world um I enjoy them but if somebody came and said, Mary um the Sisters of Mercy have decided to put you into here and that would be better for you to be able to manage how you've been and I would like to go and do and I'd be wanting. I would not want to lose some people there.
So you are comfortable here now?
Yes.
I don't think they would move you from here!
Oh I don't think that. I think that the whole thing of the dementia thing is um it's there that's what somethings hit you on…
It's with you all the time!
Yeah it's no use trying to get what you can't get.
Get what you can't get… can you try and explain that to this slow person?
Oh no it's um what I would like would be um to live with the one person.
That is very clear! So that one person looks after you and there is no one else around and so that it is a lot quieter?
Yeees! Yes and I'm. I suppose it comes out of I live with a lot of people and I don't like living with a lot of people and I'm living with people who are mostly people who would have no um who haven't got much stuff in their head anyway the main thing is that I've just got…um…I'm not really really

bad about it sad about but I don't know don't know. It's more ...

I have problems about um praying ...
Why do you have problems about praying?
Well I don't get anywhere there is prayer ...
Like you do in the convent?
Yeah.
You don't get anywhere there is quiet? Your memory is shot and you can't remember prayers or how to pray?
I know how to pray!

Can I have a joke?
Can you have a joke?
Yes!
What kind of joke would you like?
[Silence] ... Can you hear that out there?
I can hear the visitors, yes it is quite noisy and that drives you mad doesn't it?
Yes. [Silence]

I suppose I am grateful my problem is not is not um pain
Physical pain?
Physical pain ...
Why are you grateful?
Because I'm apart from having a bad leg which isn't a great one you know you've got pain and that is dreadful and ...
Don't you think emotional and mental pain is just as difficult to live with?
Yes but um most people to me anyway I don't know ...
It's a hard one that one!
It is.
You have people who are in emotional, mental and spiritual pain and some of them commit suicide because they cannot stand it any longer. The same can be said for physical pain. But pain is pain whether it is emotional or physical and I don't think it can be judged one worse than the other but both are very difficult to live with.

I think one of my pains is is my knowing is lost. I could um do a lot with my head inside and now it's ... It's not that I've lost the lot but it is hard to get at it.
And you're saying that is painful?

Yes it's a loss but I'm sure... the fact that you've helped me in this way is amazing and I don't know.
Let's just say that we are both amazing women!
[Laughter]
Cause we are!

I had a dream last night did I tell you that?
No.
Well it wasn't a dream last night but it happened last night. When you went out I got to there were one woman in that um she's nice to me and I thought I had to get up and you'll have to get other people helping me and I didn't sleep all night I think and I think this was a silly thing I um I don't know what it is I do but I like to have somebody round me so if someone is not there... what I did last night I don't think I was asleep last night um I lay in bed all my night and that was because I was getting into bed and out of it. I woke up and I got a shock and there is another building and um I ended up doing what was right doing in it. That's mad! Anyway here I am.

[We sang the chorus from the hymn Here I am Lord, it is I Lord, and at the end Mary started to cry]

That's another thing, if I it is easy to cry but I don't make a big thing of it. Lots of things like that particular thing, I've just cried a bit and gone.
Why did it make you cry?
I don't know. I think it is I I'm not in it that's probably the thing that happened. It's a beautiful song isn't it?
Yes. It certainly moved you.
MMm-hmmm!
You miss that kind of prayer and the singing together.
Yes.
That is one of the things that I missed when I left the convent, the beautiful music and prayer. There were some beautifully creative women in Grafton who brought at lot of wonder to our prayer. There is certainly some togetherness in that kind of prayer.
Yes thinking of thinking what it is what is it there is something about me that feels I'm lost in it.

You're lost in the dementia?
No not the dementia. It is there all the time and I've often wondered if something really big happened to me when I was younger. I sing a lot

to myself but if I happen to have somebody with me want to um give the something to it um anyway I've got enough on my mind and I've got a lovely friend.

Who is a terrible singer.

[Laughter]

I'm looking forward to M. teaching us do you know that she was a teacher of music and there was um thing given to us in the down here somewhere and having her there will make it better. We are getting a thing called music something…

Music therapy?

Yeah and I could if I could get at it if someone could start it I could pick up most of it. Not good but it's there and I'm thinking that M. will be singing no doubt about that.

M. is going to come and help?

Yes I'd say so or do some work with the lady doing it.

The song that I can sing straight off get off is um now it's gone.

[Mary starts singing it's a long way to Tipperary. I join in]

What ya thinking girl?

I'd like to have a holiday. I haven't had a holiday for two years.

What about holidays?

I think I should have some.

The first question I should have asked was where do you wish to go on your holiday and what do you want to do?

I don't think that um people who have dementia should be cut off from a holiday.

Good on ya. But one of the biggest problems with people with dementia is that if we take them out of their know environment they often get more confused, they can get aggressive, anxious and fight people because they get muddled more easily because they are not around anything or anyone that they know. One of the reasons that you feel comfortable with this place now is because it is known to you. If I was to take you away from here and put you in a house that you had never seen before you would most probably get anxious, confused, frustrated, upset and you'd probably start throwing things.

Well I've done that. [Laughter]

Dementia does not preclude people going on holidays what makes it difficult is some of those things I've said.

I wouldn't go.

46

But you just said that you wanted to go on a holiday!
But I wouldn't go with someone I didn't know. For example um I heard people saying yesterday that um such and such was taking like the runners I'd take somebody who knows me. Oh well.
What would you do on a holiday Mary?
I'd have this there. Haven't you got enough energy to pick this place up and put it there and you can come with me.
So you want a different view out the window?
Yes. I might see somebody again. I think that is what is coming up with the sisters the nuns who are going around it is only a day is not just to meet the people again.
One thing about dementia it cuts you off from others.
I don't mind. When I come home from the day the day we went we went right up to Grafton and back that was lovely.

I like your presence.
I'm so pleased. I like your presence too.
[Laughter]

There is a house out somewhere that I don't like it's out we are in Casino and you go from Casino away from where…
[I suggested several towns]
There is a house somewhere somebody lives in all the time. I don't know who lives in it full time. I'm letting able to let it be what it can be.
[Mary started singing]
Is that a song you know? That was a very sad thing about that man… My sister D. is one thing I am getting better into. I do have connection and one of the things I've been know is her first son I'd say he'd be about 45, 50 he's been all over the world he um when he finished school he didn't go to be this or that he went from um he went places in various places and he had something going about something in the head I'd talk to him he went everywhere from top to bottom on push bike and he did things about I think it is in his head the things that you get he does things like we names do this is what you can get into yourself not Australia—Ireland what it is up to at the present time is D. is waiting for him to give the word. He should really write his life. He's lived his life inside things…
So he is a very spiritual bloke?
Oh yes and he ah he'd go to a place where he knew they were people doing thinking things…
Think Tank organisations?

Yeah yes and D. said the other day she said he doesn't want to move out of losing this way of being um that will be very interesting if they marry and get children.

Their children will probably be geniuses.

His friend is an Irish girl and they are somehow connected. They don't live together and the girl that he has lives down in my favourite place in Ireland. It is where the river the river meets the sea.

Would you like one more trip to Ireland?

I'll never have it but I can be more able to look to it people have gone to Ireland and talked to me and people who've things have happened in Ireland.

And the memory takes you there!

Yes and I remember now I not remember—I didn't know this now I will remember I have Irish eyes.

[Sang When Irish eyes are smiling] [Laughter]

Do the angels sing?

I'd reckon better than us!

Do you know that I have Irish Eyes?

Yes you have beautiful blue Irish Eyes. We've had this conversation about eight times.

Aw! Don't be silly!

[Laughter]

No we've only had it four times!

Two!

Two! Yeah I think it is only two. You'd be right. I'd be stirring you again.

When am I going to be able to thank you enough for what you are doing? What you are doing for me?

Our friendship is enough. Why do I need thanks when I have the most precious thing in the world and that is your love?

I want to know how I could um thank you.

Oh! You could put $100k in my bank account. That will be fine.

[Laughter]

I'll put all mine in for you. I don't need it.

Well the trouble is about that Mary is that you wouldn't be able to do it now because it could be said that you are not legally competent.

That's right.

You could tell them anything you want and they would say yes Mary and do nothing. Which is right because you could be manipulated at this stage of your life.

Yes.

A lot of older people are persuaded to hand over their money and their belongings by unscrupulous people. It is an ugly side of humanity. Back to the main issue Mary, what would I need? I've had your friendship since I was 13 years old when you first plonked me on the head with that piece of chalk.

[Laughter]

What a wonderful thing to have given you.

Exactly! What a great memory that is.

I don't believe it!

You've got dementia. How would you know! You can't remember anything. I could tell you anything and you would have to believe me wouldn't ya!

[Laughter]

Actually that story is very true - it is a significant memory of my childhood. And I was um…

You were a math teacher trying to get my attention.

I didn't…

Why do you want to give me something? What do you want to do for me when we are both sharing something precious?

Yes it is there.

You could put in a good word with God for me.

Okay.

Tell him not to make tests…

Too many more…

… challenges…

No, no, no um… (Mary made a cranky sound) um what do you get you get?

A belly ache, challenges, pain.

What's the pain?

I've got an injury.

Injury, okay we'll leave it at that.

I have no idea what you are talking about. Are you dementing?

I beg your pardon?

Are you dementing?

No I'm trying I know you get a lot of pain but but pain also has something else in it it's…

I get exhausted all the time and that can often be difficult within itself and to cope with. It is difficult when you are in pain and you lose that energy level and sometimes it is really hard to think too. There are a lot of things that go with it that make it really hard to live and work with.

But that is my life.

How many children does D. have?
Two. A. and G. We have some lovely photos of you with them before you lost your marbles.
Oh dear! [Laughter] There are people who would be shocked with that.
Have you had friends come along and ask how many marbles have you lost so far Mary? [Loud laughter from both]
I am such a caring sensitive friend! It is nice to be able to laugh about our illness sometimes.
Yes. Yes. And the other thing is is that the um giving away ah not giving away but give away things that's a good thing.
To be able to laugh about it. And on that note I hope you don't lose any more marbles by the time I get back.
[More laughter]

25th April 2015

I just made a decision to speak to the ladies to say look hey what, I've been in this situation for 20 years and going into not having any help. That's not right. That's not right. I had had never I was worn out trying to be nice and I think I would have at least somewhere where I could go and have a little … [Mary is emotional]

So, when I walked in upstairs you looked at me really blankly and asked are you my friend?

I knew it but I um what do you call it …

A bit confused?

No. No I quickly no I looked at you and checked it that's not what …

Can you remember where I am from?

Yes. Kempsey.

Do you remember my name?

Jenny.

Yeeha!

We had a lovely gathering of the sisters from Grafton. We didn't all come but it was a gathering to enjoy and we had it in the … ah what am I saying? The inside of the convent where we worked.

Discovered that the gathering happened here at St Michaels.

It was lovely. I think there was about 25 of them gathered. It was nice. It was lovely. We had our lunch.

When did this happen Mary?

About two or three weeks ago. I wanted it because I was so lonely. There was nobody with me and I thought ask them could we have this activity. It is here where it happened. It was wonderful.

Why do you get lonely Mary?

I wasn't the same. All they are now are individuals. You know that.

The sisters?

Yes they live individually um. You had to be able to look after yourself. I couldn't. And um it was a very good thing. There are some still doing their own thing. Some down your way didn't come but that was okay. I was interested in what they were doing and where. So I had that wonderful experience. R. was great.

Do you mean that there will be people who will put this information together?

No I will put the book together. Who would you like to share it with? I thought that we could give a copy of it St Michael's here. I would only get a few copies done up. I wouldn't get a massive amount done. But we could give a copy to the Alzheimer's Association; Sisters of Mercy in Grafton, maybe your sisters would like a copy. Who else would you like to give a copy too?

I don't think I want to the thing is I am now that this is me and um I don't have to um tell my tell my yes tell my memory um stuff I ah things in time I'm taking that's that and um I haven't jumped over the um window yet and I don't think I will.

Is this talk of suicide?

No.

What do you mean by jumping out the window then, 'cause you ain't got far to fall?

No … I asked would they gather 'cause I was a bit …

Lonely?

No not lonely. Nobody was doing what I was wanting no visiting.

Maybe you were not remembering the visiting?

Nurse came into the room. Mary claps her hands to get attention

Nurse: No she is not smacking us yet, are you Mary? She probably feels like it at times!

You get so frustrated that you cannot do the things that you would like to do. That comes across on the tape.

Nurse: There are a lot of things that do Mary's head in and frustrate her.

What are you thinking?
I've settled down.
You look calmer.
Yes and that's where I've come on from where I've come into I've had a I came to that place where go and do it. You don't get um I've got all this whatever it is in these years and um nothing for it. Nobody what was happening in her. If something should be happening I should have a part in it so I you know who the other lady who has your name ... I got someone to ring her up. I had no idea that she'd be responsible weather she'd get through anyway yesterday I said to her I one of my um one of my happening things that I am not happy about and that is I've been here for 20 no yep 20 no I'm caught up.
Excuse me do you know that you were confused then?
Yep.
So you could pick out that you are confused? You've been here for about two years now.
No I've been here 20, 30, 40 years.
In the convent you mean?
Yes ... No in this place in St Michaels in where I live now. In where I live and love. I um been here to be looked after for I can't think of the number. When I came from here and the next year and the next year and the next year and the coming up one for the next year I think and I said I should somehow be more able or more I Um ... I'll work my way through this ...
What are you thinking about my friend?
I'm waiting for this song to finish [How Great thou Art] 20, 40 no how many times have I been here?
In St Michael's?
Yes.
Close to 2 years now as a patient in this nursing home.
[Laugh]
I think I've been here forever.
[Laughter]
It probably feels forever but you were also in the nursing home that had some attachment to the Grafton Dougherty's.
I've never been there.
The nursing home in Grafton?

53

No.

Never!

Never!

Okay this is where I need to tell you that you have misremembered. Okay for the simple reason is that you've completely lost the memory of spending time in the nursing home in Grafton. Do you remember spending time in the nursing home in Ulmarra?

No.

And yet I've taken you to that nursing home in Ulmarra to say goodbye to people when you were moving into the nursing home in Grafton. You spent well over twelve months there and you went from there to here. It wasn't a dementia specific unit. This one is. It also means that it is a locked unit. You cannot get out of it by yourself. That is specifically for those who go wandering. So you've been here a little less than 2 years. You've been in the convent now a long time.

No, I was not thinking of the convent at all.

Why would you think that you've been here for 40 years?

Well I I went to Grafton before that I had what you're talking about the Dougherty's that was there.

Do you remember being there?

I do and I remembered the people I liked being there.

So why did you tell me that you didn't remember it?

Oh well I'm in a mess at this present time in trying to work things out 'cause I'm wanting to do something more than I've been doing.

What can you do apart from just surviving?

Well I when I had the first thing running it was I had to do this and it just went on a they did it and when I come to this place I didn't like it no matter how much I pushed I hated it.

The noise and the people did your head in!

Anyway I saw this other I didn't do it. I wanted to say to I wanted her to it was something about nobody was not here not um in this place where I am now I felt I was so so um lost not you're not there and I what I was going to do was ask her would I be able to have um I've lost it.

You wanted to change? You wanted to go somewhere else?

No. I'm not thinking of the war. I'm thinking of the in this place there is very little in the flying in this area but one please that flies over I think I'm almost sure my nephew works there.

Yes you've told me about your nephew. He works with the aviation industry and is an aircraft controller and an engineer.

Can you write that somewhere where I can remember, keep it in my head.

I will keep on reminding you. Does it make you sad to forget things like that?
Yes and but it is not as bad
As bad as what?
I used to be and the family I could never get to ...
And you miss your family?
Yeah. D. is the next after me from where we began.
Isn't Ilene the oldest?
She died.
You are the oldest now.
And um P. is here ...

Would there be any way that you could suggest that I would get at that stuff in the reality of what is happening out there. I've heard little things going out over our heads. Not here very much but now and again you'll get one over.
Okay, if you'd spoken that in Spanish I might have had a chance of understanding it.
What?
[Laughter]
Exactly. What!
[More laughter]
I have no idea what you are talking about Mary. None of it made sense to me.
[Laughter]
Don't say that.
Why? Does that make you cranky?
Nah!
Okay it didn't make sense to me but obviously it made sense to you. I don't understand. What were you trying to say? What was the subject?
That this man who is my nephew truthfully in this area doesn't fly but is responsible ...
You want to go and see him?
I want to get information.
So is he the son of?
P. ... he is actually not P. ... to hard but it is hard to go close to the people ... um.

My family said was a genius.
I think you were a genius Mary, very very smart.
[Silence]

Do you know that they are playing Christmas Carols out there?
Yes they have got them on for the kids ... no they are not kids.

So what do you pray for?
I don't.
You don't pray. How does that make you feel?
Uuum! I think when I got stuck in the dementia I told God to look after me 'cause I'm I don't get anything in my head.
You don't remember to pray, is that what you are saying?
Yes I think so. No it's not I'm remembering its I am non its more I've said to God that I can't pray and I'll just go on and he will look after me.
So everything in your life is an eternal prayer and God is good!

Does it frustrate you that you can't you know pray or go to church or do the things that you used to do normally did as a sister of Mercy?
Yes ... the thing I said to ah ... what's your name?
Jenny.
Jenny well we have another Jenny. I um I hope I can say oh! Um ...
You'd like someone to take you to church?
Oh yes! I would like the priest to come over here and again to say mass.
Have you still got your rosary beads?
Yes
Do you know how to use them now?
No. I do I do but I don't.
Do you remember when I was in the noviciate? No ... well I used to go down onto the river bank at least once a day to not only say the rosary but to have a smoke break.
[Laughter]
So, does that frustrate that you cannot pick up the rosary beads and say the rosary?
No no it does not. I've said to God you look after me.
Sometimes I don't say the rosary I just pick up the beads and hold them and that can be comforting at times. Do you find that so?
We have the rosary here. There is rosary I don't know. I do know but I cannot put it into words.
That is part of what dementia is about.
[Mary hiccupped]
That is the alcohol you had a breakfast.
[Silence]
What no laughter!

56

Well I can laugh and see … I don't cry!

Yes you do!

I don't!

You've got dementia Mary! How would you remember?

I mean I have got dementia …

[Laughter]

I I …

A doctor did diagnose you in Grafton Mary. You and I have talked a lot about you having dementia. I also talk about the symptoms of dementia. How you were possibly going to respond over time and how you were going to lose your memory. You were going to forget who I was and how you had signed all your money over to me.

[Laughter]

Now she knows I am joking!

I feel … no I don't feel what I know is yes what I think is um I haven't I haven't had a um what would you call it … I've um done been able to be here um but I haven't I haven't help given me something that's a holiday in the head. Do you know what a holiday in the head is?

Um you want to be able to be Mary Quinn again without the dementia. You want to be able to get away from the dementia for a while. Is that what you are trying to say?

Yes. Something that …

You want to be able to speak what you are thinking, feeling.

Yes.

You are frustrated and you want a holiday in your head so that you can say those things.

Yes! Yes!

That is a very good way of saying it. I want a holiday from my pain. People talk about going on holidays and I just look at them and think but what I'd give to be able to have one or two days completely without pain. It would be like your holiday in your head. It is so frustrating isn't it?

Yes it is yes. My frustration is mostly about um this is happening to me and it is going to but I have got in the more recent time been able to put in my head it's not going to happen. It's just going to go on but I don't yeah anyway. I don't um cry very much.

No you don't. You get really teary and then you get yourself back together again.

Yeah.

You get very moved and you get tears in your eyes.

I also get angry tears.

The times that I've seen the tears it has been because you have felt something strongly passionate.

Yeah. Well do you think from your point of view would I be doing something that would help to if able to get a holiday?

If you had a holiday in your head where you became Mary Quinn again without all the associated memory and health problems I could see you going over to Ireland and having a good time over there. I could see Mary Quinn finishing her book which hopefully will get finished sometime. Um I could see Mary Quinn visiting all of her nieces and nephews and the rest of the family and I could still see Mary Quinn continuing to serve the Lord in various ways because the Mary Quinn I know is a very strong, powerful generous giving woman. And to see her brought to this state by an illness um is very distressing thing for me to see . . . let alone how it is with you.

Yes.

The other thing um in this being somewhere um out of here is I would like to use my brain I have a brain. I don't have whatever else is and I'd like to use that . . .

How would you like to use your brain Mary?

Oh to help people . . .

Physically you are stuck in this nursing home in the dementia unit. You have people caring for you. You cannot walk around.

No.

Basically your life is as an invalid and your physical wellbeing has been cut short by your illness and that is frustrating for you because you feel that you have more to offer. Is that what you are thinking?

[Strongly said] Yes! Um! The other person who runs this place does nothing for me.

Let's look at that comment and then ask what can she do for you? What can anyone do for you? Maybe prayer would be good.

Yes and I do pray . . . different!

Yeah. I mean I feel myself not useless but . . . I visit you as often as I can and the reason I do that is I love you and because you are a significant woman in my life and have been so since I was a child. You have been an inspiration to me and you always will be. I asked you about writing your story about your fight with dementia because I felt that the Mary Quinn I knew would be fascinated with that kind of story. What I am discovering is that the Mary Quinn I know is still there, and you might feel as if you are not offering anything to the world or to the community because of your present state, but by speaking to me about the frustration and where you are at and what you are feeling you are giving. You might not see it, but your story is going to get out there and it is something that people can listen to and hear and marvel at the faith of a woman called Mary Quinn. You have an amazing faith.

I've been too serious for too long. I have to tell a joke now...
[Laughter]
Can you understand what I am saying?
I can.
You may feel as if your life is worthless; you might feel as if you've got nothing left to offer, but I am saying to you that we are doing something together.
I don't feel that I am an invalid. [Laugh] I feel mad about the way this operates.
The dementia?
Yes.
You got a right to be mad about the way it operates.
I was so mad after I left the first thing that was the second thing that happened and I was in a place in Grafton down the line you just got it said your prayers looked let them look after you feed you and there it was I later on I thought silly woman why did you do that. That was just wonderful it was the thing that for me um and I don't I feel that I don't do anything and the other place in Grafton I could do for the people there. They were nice people and I can't do that here. I like the people who look after me and I am grateful and I feel that is all I can do.
Now you are emotional.
[Crying] just walking around don't even know what and that is why I wanted to get some of the nuns back. Nobody here bothers to try and get me here.

I'm grateful about the fact that I can listen, it's not listening it's hearing...
[Sat in comfortable silence]
I'm glad I've got you around. [Laughs]
What is so funny?
Well we have a capacity to laugh, talk about reality.

26th April 2015

Jesus went where?
What? They always want to be Jesus instead of waiting for Jesus. It's quiet funny. No it is not funny at all.
Do you think people were abusing Jesus in church this morning?
Yes!
They were! And why did it make you cranky?
Well the girl who took me over to the church organised me to sit in the place and Jesus looked after his people and they wanted to be with him... I don't know it off by heart... God being the...
Good shepherd?
... the Good Shepherd, the Good Shepherd and somebody else says we were the people that God had as people...
We are his sheep, his flock.
Yes and as soon as the next one comes and does it, the next one comes and does it, and the next one comes and does it, and the next one comes and does it. It was...
Irritating?
Irritating yes! If they really wanted to do something with Jesus um it looked more like 'look at me, look at me!'
Is what you talking about is a bit like the rich man in the temple putting himself out there so everyone can see how holy he is and looks for rewards in this life? Not like the people who do good deeds on the quiet.

Yep.

Don't you think that religions are a bit like those men in the temple?

Hey! I don't know.

Because you are walking around in today's society. You used to walk around in a habit but now you walk around with a cross and you know that they are sisters and that they have given their lives to Jesus so we know that they are doing the work of the Lord. They are not doing it in secret or quiet but they are doing it so that everyone sees what they are doing. Aren't they bit like the rich man in the temple?

[Silence]

Are you going to throw something at me now? You are giving me a dirty look.

No. I don't know. It's like um I have [Confused gabble]…anyway it nice to have you here.

You are not going to answer my question are you?

What?

About whether you are like the rich man in the temple?

[Silence]

My answer to that is no you are not like the rich man in the temple because the rich man in the temple wants his rewards now and you Mary living your life as an example and are not after earthly rewards.

I'm after…

What are you after if you are not after earthly rewards?

I'm after um um…

I thought that you wanted to dance with the Lord in heaven.

Um that is interesting. Being a teacher which was my vocation put me into contact with people so that I could let them know that there is a God…

So your aim was to teach people by example and what a great job you've done even if you had to throw chalk at them.

[Laughter]

This house, I haven't been here for yonks.

This room?

Yes.

This is your bedroom. Do you not remember that this is your bedroom?

I'm not here I'm over in the dementia…

The dementia wing?

Um.

What do you think this wing is?

It is for the ladies who do their bit … um …
Would you believe me if I told you that you actually are in the dementia wing and that you are in your bedroom?
[Silence]
How do I know? See all the pictures on the wall?
Yes.
They are the ones that I took and put there for you about six months ago.
Oh!
Do you remember that?
Well I know they were there.
And there is the drawing of yours and my hand up behind you.
Yeah I know that … do I?
Do you? You sleep in that bed there. It doesn't look familiar to you at all?
Now it does. I don't think what I do.
Are you feeling a little confused today?
No I was a bit cranky about the earlier thing the church stuff and I was worried that
I'd …
Miss me?
Miss you … no that you'd have to wait for me.

Last night the other one of your name …
Jenny.
Umm she said yes to my wanting to talk to the big wigs about getting some time off.
Out of here?
Yes.
Where do you wanna go?
I've been thinking. Would you have any ideas?
Well Mary I do not think there is anywhere you could go unless it was to another nursing home. Who would look after you?
[Silence]
I hadn't thought of that.
Because you need help showering and mobilizing and all the sisters are getting rather fragile themselves and I cannot help because of my injury.
I wouldn't look for time. I'd do it in days.
So you'd go out for day trips.
Yeah. Go down the town and come back with somebody.
What would you do down town?
Nothing I'm just saying it's the way for example you know where the road

goes that way?
Tenterfield?
Yes in that area there some things about airs flying but not me.
Airports?
Yeah.
So you want to get on a plane?
No. To go out to where they land and take off…

Garbled conversation regarding nephew.

Mary can I say that you are suffering from dementia.
[Laughter]
Am I.
I just thought I'd let you know that 'cause you've told me this story about your nephew about 10 times.
That is not true!
It is true.
Well why don't you tell me to shut up?
Why you might tell me something new every time you tell me the story you never know.
Anyway I'll leave the other… the other… what's your name?
Who me?
Yes.
Geraldine.
Who?
Geraldine.
You're not.
Kay.
Are you?
Am I?
No you are not.
Robyn
No.
Lorraine
You are not.
Jenny
Jenny yes. There is another Jenny. She is ready to do something for me.
Shoot you?
[Laugh] No. I'd leave it to her. She might take me somewhere. To give me a visit…
Do you remember that I said I had something… dementia

Because you kept on repeating the story about your nephew?
[Laugh]
Let's forget that.
Yes.
And everything I know I forget. But I don't believe that.
Why don't you believe that you forget it when you obviously accept the fact that you've got dementia and dementia is about memory loss?
Why don't I what?
So are you going to answer my question?
What was it?
If you believe that you've got dementia and you agree that you've got dementia and the associated memory loss that comes with dementia, why then don't you believe when I say to you that you've told me about your nephew and what he does 10 times. Why don't you believe that?
I don't think. It's not that I tell you that many times, it is there ever anything got out of it. If I don't think or want and you know that I talk about it.
It is very hard to keep yourself clear?
It is. But if I'd do that nobody is really interested in what I think or what I am doing.
Do you think that is because of your dementia?
Yes.
So they think you are slow now?
I beg your pardon? No because they don't the people who love me um and um listen at least it's nothing.
Do you think what you say is nothing?
Yes!
Why?
[Silence]
How do you know that? Just because you've got dementia it means that what you say means nothing?
Cause you keep telling me [laughter] that I say I keep doing things
Yes.
Well it is the same thing.
No it is not! You keep repeating yourself.
Yes.
Okay that is part of dementia but what you have to say is not nothing. You have something to say and whether you repeat it five times or a thousand that doesn't matter, it is still important. There are things you say that you don't repeat that are important and are very moving. Can you understand the difference?

64

I do not think so.
Okay. You tell me about your nephew.
Yes
You've told me about your nephew many times.
Yes.
It might not have been ten times but it is pretty close up there.
Yeah! Yeah!
That's fine but that is only about your nephew. Okay. We talk about things like the dementia; how you feel; about what it is like when you were in the convent; we talk about your vocation; your relationship with God; how you want to help people now and how you've helped people in the past and all the stuff that you say, a lot of it is wise and a lot of it is very moving; and a lot of it is amazing for a person who is suffering from dementia. Right?! So you've got a lot to say that is not nothing. You've always got something to say and I will always listen . . .
Hum!
. . . because I am amazed at what you have to say.
Yeah.
Although I do not want to hear much more about your nephew!

No what I was looking at wasn't . . . um . . . isn't what I'm saying 'cause you hear it. But what I am trying to get is I want to have something that I can get done or from somebody in this house who will give me an ear who sees that that I want to do something. I have to keep saying it. I'm . . .
Do you feel useless Mary?
Yes! I keeping saying to myself 'leave it to God'.

What would you like to do if you got the opportunity?
To what?
I don't know. What would you like to do?
I would like this . . . what's her name? She has said she would um go to the higher person and see what we could do and I have a lot of my memory of my um family in this part of where it is here out there that fellow there this woman is round just my what's a name Patty is just round the corner . . .
This is very hard on you Mary.
There are two I would have told you about this before. Most of Patty's P's children are coming through. I was the one who did it.
You used to do a lot for her children.
That's right because Patty P couldn't do it and there are things I want to do if I can.

You are very good with children.
There are two...those two girls young ones...I would like to see if I could get in touch with them and talk to them for a day...I might be able to do something if someone was helping me.

Do you like watching airplanes take off?
Haven't seen them much. What has this got to do with dementia?
Nothing it's just that you talked about planes earlier and I couldn't understand the context. Sometimes you ask questions that are really quite sharp. I mean I ask you about a plane and you want to know what it's got to do in relation to your dementia so...
Grafton has a lot of bits in it and one is Grafton and the other one is where, where...
You mean like Maclean and Ulmarra?
Yeah what is the name of where um the um next to us I'm not in Grafton I am in another place around here.
Junction Hill?
No. no. no!
Casino.
Yes Casino and I don't know why I wanted to say that. Anyway I'm not in Grafton. Casino, Casino there is a little house out the road and it's a...there is another one out in the wind in Casino and that's where a lot of dementia...I get thrown out there if I've done something bad which I have I've screamed at someone or knocked someone over or whatever and uh I don't like it. I'd rather stay here in Casino. The other people who are in this state drive me crazy.
[Laughter]
Who are suffering from dementia?
Yes.
[Laughter]
That is really hilarious.
What do you mean?
It is just really funny that someone who has got dementia does not like living with someone who has got dementia. It is just very amusing.
If you had it would you like to live with others with it?
Mary, I don't know.

You can't tell me that it's all wonderful what you do for me.
Sometimes it is really hard speaking with you because I get really sad. But I do not have to live in the same community with you and the others

who share dementia. If you didn't like the noise in this place and I can understand that because it does get noisy ... I myself am a quiet person and like to be by myself so if I was in a unit such as this I would spend most of my time closing the doors. That's probably [laugh] where my dementia would go, I'd run around closing doors all day.

[Laughter]

And if mine had a lock on it I would lock it too. I think I don't have dementia at the moment. I think that dementia is one of the cruellest illnesses anyone can ever have. But once that you've got it fully completely without thought and you basically do not know anyone and cannot talk that's okay because you do not remember but when you are going through the memory loss and you still are aware of who you are and who your friends are and what is happening to you I think that is terribly cruel. Don't you?

Grunt!

What was your question? I cannot remember it.

Don't know.

[Laughter]

If I had dementia I do not think I would be as brave as you Mary.

But I've got people behind me including you.

You also have God. I know that.

There is a young woman who has taken ... has stuck to me. It is awful.

Why? What does it mean that she has stuck to you? She doesn't want to leave you? Do you think it is because she thinks you are an amazing woman?

No ... I think she thinks I should look after her ... she drives me crazy and I feel bad.

In that case have another drink of chocolate milk.

Thank you.

[Laughter]

You are supposed to drink milk not snort it.

[Laughter]

What are you going to do when you go home?

I do a lot of writing. Ah! I work for an organisation that works with older people and those with dementia and I do other voluntary work in the community.

Where is it?

It is in Kempsey. For somebody who doesn't work, I seem to be flat out all the time but that's because I have to do things slowly these days because

of the injury. But I still do things. It's important that I continue to do things because if I don't I'll become a total and utter hermit and not do anything for anybody and die sooner than I mean to. But I won't do it. I'll let you do it first.
[Laughter]
Don't you dare!
No I won't. I promise you. God will look after us.
Yes. I'm not thinking of anything at all about ...

You're irritable!
What?
Your arms are moving around like anything. Are you feeling cranky?
No there is little chips here.
[I removed the crumbs]
Oh! Is that better?
Well yes.
So stop moving you look like you've got worms.
I might have.
[Laughter]
Please God!
Please God what?
Don't give me worms.
[Laughter]
There is a genius in there ... talking about a man who works here with those with dementia. Oh well I'll let you know what Jenny gets me for my holiday.
She might get you a teacher to teach you how to surf.

I don't know ... You know the queen who died?
The queen who died ... You mean Queen Elizabeth I?
No the one who ... that Australian ...
The one that what?
There was a Queen, there was a queen who was in Australia.
Oh the one from what country was she from?
She died ... and then that Henry ... no it is not Henry it's the brother ... what was his name?
Sorry no idea my history is not all that sound. Thanks for loaning me your bed.
You look very nice in it.
[Laughter]

I'll give you my keys and you can go on home to my place.
Harry who can over from England. That was a very sad thing.
They reckon it was very moving the Anzac day ceremonies.
[A long break in the conversation]

What are those chocolates named?
Wagon wheels. There is also a packet of mint slice in the fridge.
What time is it?
About 11.30 am. Do you feel tired?
No. Thank God. Well it is one thing…

30th May 2015

I came into Mary's bedroom this day to find her lying on the bed. She appeared to be not in a good space. I was told by the nurses that she lost her temper at breakfast. This manifested by Mary spitting her tablets at the nurses and throwing her water glass across the room. When she opened her eyes she immediately snarled at me asking me who I was. I replied that I was her visitor. She smiled and we started to talk.

So you are saying that you are mad?
It's not ... there is something wrong with me. You have two heads!
Well thank you very much.
I see it.
So there is something wrong with your eye sight for one thing if you think I've got two heads. So why did you just nearly cry?
You are about the only person I know.
I'm about the only person you know! What about R.?
No unfortunately.
Why don't you know R.?
Huh?
Why don't you know R.?
Well she is just down the road and never comes to see me.
Who am I?
Jenny.

Who was the last person to visit you?
There is some still in girls work ... and some of them love me.
So you feel as if you are not being loved?
Yes! I have no mother. I have no father. I have no sisters and no family.
What about P.?
Never says anything.
Do you think anything of this is to do with your dementia?
Could be.
It could be that you cannot remember people coming and seeing you.
[Silence]
The feeling I'm getting and the vibe I'm getting is that you are feeling really cranky and frustrated and angry. Is that true?
I'm ... say that again.
The feeling I'm getting is that you are feeling cranky and frustrated and angry and lonely.
Lonely.
You are feeling lonely!
Terribly lonely.
[Mary sighed]
Bugger!
Nowhere no one.
No one has seen you. So where did these lollies come from if no one has visited you?
You.
No I did not buy them. Where did these mint slices come from? And look at all the lollies up here.
The workers bring me them. I thought you were gone.
Gone where? Died?
No ... just not coming.
Look at those hands, the hands that I drew for us, you and me.
Are they still there?
Yes those hands are still there on the wall. Every time you think I'm not coming, you look at those hands and know that I will be coming. Sometimes it might not be every month because of other commitments, but I'll be still coming.
I'm totally ... I don't know what it is ...

Am I up in the air today? Am I lying ...
You are on a bed.
I am on a bed.

D., my brother just texted me and said to give you his love.
Thank you and how is the baby?
The baby is seven years old.
[Laughter]
So he is in school!

Why did you ask about euthanasia when I first came in?
I um! There are two people I've heard about it euthanasia … there is a lady here. She doesn't know where she is or what she is doing and she tells me she had to um um … look after her mother and next would be she says she um looked after her father and another time she had to … she thinks it would be better is she didn't have to suffer. She didn't use the term euthanasia …
So they wanted them to die comfortably?
Yes along the lines of … I'm saying this stuff about what is going on and here is me not being able to manage it.
Is there a problem without not being able to manage it?
I think so.
As far as I reckon, you manage it how you manage it. I mean I don't think that you have just got dementia Mary. You've also probably got cardiac issues and then there was the melanoma on your back that left a rather large scar and knocked you around. I'd say that your body is not working real well at the moment.

I don't know why I did it but I but I've been in my head thinking that this part of me … The cancer on your back?
There is something about it still in my breast I don't think it is right. I'm half thinking that it has come back again so I told some of the girls and I sorta but I think the doctor is a baby. Anyway I will keep thinking about what to do.
Well let's say that if you did have breast cancer what would you do about it? You are in your mid-eighties would you decide to have treatment to get rid of it or would you say I've got it so be it and not have treatment?
No. I don't know 'cause I only I can't touch it.
Does it hurt?
Yes. One part of it. We won't think about that. What am I doing up on this?

You were on the bed when I got here. Do you wish to get up?
Yes. No I don't!
You must have been feeling a bit tired after breakfast.
Well I say stupid things. I don't know. [Mary started to sound upset] The day before yesterday I went to someone is a fellow who ah who does things in

the getting oh I can go like that at him and he puts one of those things ... it's mad ... it's mad. Can I have a cuddle?
Of course.

Mary has never asked me for a cuddle before. I gave her a cuddle.

I'm out of it.
Why do you think you are out of it?
Oh because when what I think when I get in you know the people who come and put you there and put you there it is all silly and it must be me because they are not people who are silly.
Would you call it being silly or would you think it is because you are unwell?
I'm cranky.
You're cranky. Well I figured that out. Why are you cranky?
I don't know.
You seem frustrated about something when I walked in.
I'm worried about that.
About being cranky?
Yeah.
Cranky that you might hurt somebody?
Oh well I'm telling people they're silly, they're not going to be there and it's mad. I can't be nice to people. Except you and one of the girls.
One of the nurses here?
Yes.
Why can't you be nice?
Cause I think the people who are working for working for me here are are not my people. I I'm actually here, I don't know why they have got me up here.
Probably because you are cranky and they put you on the bed to try and calm down.
Could you ... would there be time to ask you is that how they are with me? I don't know anybody's name.

I walked out of the room to ask the nurses what happened with Mary that morning.

Did you get anything from it?
I did.
It's the dementia isn't it?
I'd say so.
Am I really up here?
You put yourself up there. They just helped you up there. You spat your tablets and threw you water cup across the room in frustration.

Yeah ... so that's the dementia?

Yes that is the dementia.

Oh God!

You cannot help it Mary. How can you help illness?

I don't consider it ...

You don't consider it an illness?

Yes.

Well I would suggest that I get my walking stick and beat you with it.

[Laughter]

Don't please.

Well then you need to listen when I say that it is part of the dementia.

[Mary nods]

And there is not a great deal that you can do about it.

Okay.

Except to say that God is good. This is part of my illness and I have to accept it.

Yes.

It doesn't mean that you have the right to go and beat all the nurses up and throw your tablets at them every day.

Yeah.

Sometimes you lose control and there is not a lot you can do about it.

Yeah. Okay the other thing that might have some adverse um something good would be if you could walk over to where R. is or drive.

I could never look after myself. There are sisters that and R. is one of them confusion. Tell them what I want to do and it went out of my head.

Bugger!

Bugger!

Your hands are very soft Mary.

I hope there is something wrong with me.

You hope there is something wrong with you. Is that what you just said?

I think I did but I didn't mean it.

[Laughter]

Are you sick of living Mary?

No. No I don't want to, I don't want to die or go to heaven just yet. I'm lost! Totally lost. Does that make any sense?

I believe it does and it is a horrible place to be. You have no idea what your body and brain is doing to you. Mary Quinn is not there and you cannot understand what is happening.

Yeah.

Do you think that is what you are saying by being lost?

And I am not able, like I wanted to talk to the sister who is in charge and I just cannot get it in my mind no…

You are not able to tell it to say it?

Yeah, yeah, and I can't take you with me. I don't know anybody in my family or any [Mary breaks down and cries]

I can cry now. I didn't used too once upon a time. Can you help me how can I go out? No I can I know I am not going out. I can't do it but…

You've had enough of the struggles?

… there is no one around to put their hand in mine. I think that lady used to help and I'd love to get one of the nuns to do that for me.

Just to hold your hand?

I cannot do that with people who have to work. Some people don't want to do that. I wonder would it be a good help to get a person who is not um working and puts my hand in theirs.

I don't like getting into my feet but when I get there it is okay.

Are you talking about feet or shoes?

I beg your pardon?

Are you talking about feet or shoes?

Shoes. No I think it is feet.

Where is the nurse?

She is busy with someone else. I spoke to her. She is not upset with you about what happened.

What did she say?

I said that you were on the bed and were wondering why you were there and that she appears to be cranky and frustrated. She told me that you had spat your tablets and thrown the mug. She said she understood your frustration.

I am on top.

You are on top of your bed.

I've cried. Whatever crying is. It runs down my cheek and that is awful.

What is so wrong with crying?

I don't know. I've never cried until now. I'm not a crying person.

So maybe it is something that the Lord is teaching you at this time in your life.

[Silence]

I wish I could be you. I could go away and be happy.

I don't think you could be happy being somebody else. Do you?

No. I don't know. I think that one of the things that is hard on me in the 'demuntia' we are in two... I don't know what it is there's the people who have the dementia there is one lot that is just ordinary people and we do what our you know we do the normal things that people would do um and the other part is 'Oh my God' they... put your hand on my forehead please. What would you say?

You are not hot. Your skin is a bit dry.

The people other ones [sigh] their mad! They are not mad but they are like the birds, like birds up there in the air and they roam around screaming and making the strangest noises. [Mary made a noise to demonstrate]

They'll all think I am like that out there now.

You really don't like noise do you?

No I don't.

Are the birds out there irritating?

No it is the people out there; the poor people who have dementia. In my head I've put them in a better place. They are probably more wise and more sensible than I am. But the noise!!!

You cannot cope with the noise that they make.

Yeah... well what some of them make. It is like one of them is a chicken.

A chicken?

Yes.

[I started cackling]

[Laughter]

Yes that is exactly it.

I'd love to go around and see the sisters who are able to look after themselves but I do the opposite. I can't, I can't, I can't! That's my problem. I can't do it. I can't do it. I can't do it. I can't do it. I can't do it.

I can't do things half the time either.

Yeah.

You are such a friend.

Thank you. So are you.

I can't be now.

What do you mean you can't be now?

Well that is how I look at it.

I'm gonna wop you with this walking stick!

[Laughter]

What for?

Because of that comment. You say you cannot be my friend anymore.
No. No. No. That is not what I said.
What did you say?
Um! Oh did I do that? No isn't that awful …
You might think you have got nothing to offer Mary but you do. You are still my friend. I still love you and I still love being with you. You might be sick but you are still my mate. Now do I still need to wop you with my walking stick?
No I am I might be thinking I but I know I'm not but under that I am thinking I've got nothing …
To offer?
Yeeeah!
I worried about Mary Quinn.
Well Mary Magdalene Quinn is unwell.
Yes thank you.

I was surprised that you remembered that you had talked about euthanasia.
Why?
Because your memory is poor at times.
Well one of the things that I think there is something about having … memory loss is can sometimes pick up when I am thinking somewhere like the lady the girl um … who looked after her mother and father. I can remember which like she talked about how terrible it was to watch her husband die.
It is horrible to watch people die but I have also found it to be moving and an honour to be with someone when they are dying.
Oh yes. I was with I …

Another patient with severe dementia walked into the room. Mary got a little irate but was able to calm down pretty quickly.

I'm sad about her.
She has made you cranky in the past. She gets cranky also. That is part of her dementia.
I'm amazed how far back in time can be sung about. Isn't it amazing?
Well you look at the song Amazing Grace, it was written in the 18th Century.
Yes but these other things go way back beyond that. [Said with conviction] I like that other song.
I started singing 'By the rivers of Babylon'. That one?
Yes. How long does Babylon go back?
It was mentioned in the Old Testament so pretty old. I don't even know where it is on the map. You're a geography teacher you tell me.

Don't know that one.
Ah bugger! Did Moses pass through Babylon?
[Shrug]

Now I'm up on the top?
No you are on the ground floor. Can you see the grass out there?
Yes and I'm over there.
Yes you are in your bedroom.
My bedroom in not on that level.
Your bedroom is on the ground floor. You go upstairs for activities including prayers.
Oh God I didn't know I did that.
You do it every Sunday I think for prayer anyway.

Nurse comes into the room.

I wish someone would come along and throw me away.

Nurse: We are not going to do that.

I could throw you. Where would you like me to throw you?
In heaven.
You want to be thrown into heaven?
I would like what's happening at the very second, what's looking for me this time is where the hell am I.
Where the hell am I now?
Yeah.
Physically?
Physically.
Physically you are in St. Michaels, Casino. I don't know the name of the street sorry.
Yes.
You've been here for close on two years now. Um and you are in the dementia unit and you are on the ground floor.
They all ... I ah I dislike the way they organised the dementia people.
In what way?
I have said sat on the back at me sitting on a something for um I am wanting and I lied in a night with my back behind me earlier on um I think it is supposed to be you're in the dementia area and I cannot manage them. I more than once I have have lied on a thing on the ground for the night.
So you slept on the floor?
Yeah.

Is that because you have fallen?
I don't know. The what comes in it's a beautiful little place but I get so angry because I lie on my back and go down to the next thing. Anyway. The best thing to do is to say well I can't understand it and just take it.
The problem with that Mary is you'll make that decision that you are just going to let it lie and you cannot do anything about it and that's probably the smartest thing to do then all of a sudden five minutes later you've forgotten than you have made that decision and then you start to worry again…
Okay.
… and that's part of the dementia so it is going to … the worse part about it is it is going to keep on happening.
Yeah!
And you can't really accept it or not accept it because you will forget that you've accepted or not accepted it. That is part of your problem with you illness and I suspect that is what makes you so angry and so frustrated because you had such an analytical mind.
What is that?
That is what your mind used to be like. You used to be able to analyse/ study people and their personalities. Now your mind is not working the way it used to. It is one of the cruellest things that could have happened to you.
Okay.

You start snoring and I am going to stick my finger in your ear.
[Laughter]
It is lovely to have you here.
It is lovely to be here with you.
There would be plenty of people who do not have a lot of assistance so I better stop making silly mistakes.
What do you think a silly mistake is?
Oh I get up and go to breakfast and I can't follow what we get for breakfast.
It confuses you?
Yes and I scream out at … just bad …
Um that is not silly. That is part of the illness Mary. It is very frustrating and very 'crankifying' and you cannot do a great deal about it when it is part of the illness.
Yeah!
It is Mary Quinn at war with Mary Quinn?
Yeeees. She was a nice woman once.

[Laughter]

Do you mean there was a time when she wasn't?

Oh I am going to smack you!

[Laughter]

"She was a nice woman once!!!" Oh that is funny Mary. I've always thought you were a nice woman and I still think you are a nice woman and you are still extremely entertaining.

[Mary pretends to go for my throat with her hands]

Just let me get out with this bit; from the dementia I mean. Oh please God I hope he decides to cheer me up. I'll be right for a pretty good night. It's right.

Are you happy anymore?

I beg your pardon?

Are you happy anymore?

Why are we both grinning like idiots?

Beg your pardon?

Why are we both grinning like idiots?

[Laughter]

Because we are.

[Laughter]

Well now I know I'm on the level I wanted to be on. I won't be up on the upper one. And I'm sure I'll get you over if anything happens.

If they don't there will be bloody hell to pay.

Thank you friend.

You are welcome friend. "May the Lord bless you and keep you and hold you in the palm of his hand."

And yours. Amen.

Amen.

There are lots of things I could say and do. This is not the way my life goes. It is the demuntia … um the dementia [said with a grin]. So I can't go out and say I'll go and visit so and so, I go and do this and that … it is all what what what inside. And I suppose when anything happens that's the anger. Why the hell …

I think that you've always had a bit of anger in you?

Have I?

You've lost your temper occasionally, I thought. But it was controlled. Some people really bugged you and made you angry or some people did something stupid. I don't think you could abide incompetence and laziness.

Oh! I thought that I was the lazy one.

I'm gonna smack you. [Laughter]

Let me say it another way—you didn't suffer fools gladly is how I would describe it. But you were not someone who took your anger out on other people whereas the dementia is making you frustrated and making you angry. You are not well enough to take your anger outside and kick something. What I'm saying is that you cannot get away from it.

Yeesss!

And because you cannot get away from it the people who are standing there in front of you are the nurses and they will take the brunt of that frustration. I would say that you are gonna ... the truth is that you are going to get angry again. And somewhere in that damaged brain of yours if you can think well yes I am going to get angry, I accept that so instead of throwing things at the nurses, just throw it on the floor.

Um!

You don't want to hurt anyone so throw it on the floor and that might help you relieve a bit of your frustration.

Well that is what I did this week. It goes too much for me.

It is very upsetting for you because this is not Mary Magdalene Quinn?

Yeah!

I'm gonna smack you now.

I'll beat you to it.

You are blaming yourself for something that you shouldn't be blaming yourself for.

Yeah. I'll try.

You'll do more than try Ms Quinn. You will do it!!!!

What was that? I'm not Mrs Quinn.

I said Ms. You said that to me once. I think it was to do with math and I said 'I'll try Sr Joseph' and you responded by saying in a very authoritarian voice 'you'll do more than try Miss Clarke'.

[Laughter]

I was amused with the fact that I was doing the best I could and no amount of pushing me was going to make me do any better. I was useless at maths and I haven't improved much since. I hope that I improve because in my next life I want to be a star ship pilot.

Oh! Do you think there is going to be another life?

I think so. You could be Sr Mary of the Airwaves and I could drive you everywhere in my starship.

Suuure!

You could be a missionary to another planet.

I don't think so.

One of the sad things. No not sad. I don't know but I don't, I'm not able to get these young people in my life getting…
You cannot participate by seeing them?
That's right. Often in days go over some not big oh mills planes…

Gotta go, not feeling to well. Do you want some KFC?
Oh no don't bother.
You sure? I bring it every other Sunday that I come in.
You do? I don't remember.
Oh Mary, you must be suffering from dementia darling.
Yeees.
Terrible thing.
[Laughter]
Be good my child.
Geez, take all the fun outta life why don't ya.
I'll see you tomorrow. And remember it is not your fault.

31st May 2015

So would I make a good prostitute?
Yes I think you could.
I could? Interesting.
Where did they bury Mary?
Mother Mary, Jesus' mother?
No um Mary Magdalene.
I think it was France. Or at least that is what the scholars believe. So why are you interested in her at the moment?
Um ... because I've just been um thinking knowing that Mary Magdalene was my that was the name I was given?
Yes.
And I always liked her because she was the one who came out of the when Jesus was pulled out of ... I thought it was a nice thing to be doing. She was the one who the first one to when Jesus was coming back from wherever he was and I like what they say about her in the ... I really don't have my head!
[Mary makes frustrated sound]

Morning tea arrived.

You are not going to have biscuits! You've just had KFC. Pity you cannot remember it because you enjoyed it.
[Mary becomes agitated]
You are getting irritated with the noise?

Yes.
I would get frustrated if it is happening all the time.
Yes. A couple of the a very very noisy...
[There was a lot of noise from one particular patient in the background]
She is very noisy.
But she is very happy.
Do you want to go to your bedroom to get away from the noise?
Yes.

Physically I am stuffed but spiritually and emotionally I am okay. It gets to me sometimes because I am always in pain but other than that I am pretty good. You! How are you feeling?
I'm okay I really am. I am not being bashed around or anything like that but I cannot manage my like how I... there is so much that I cannot do that I could do.
In the past?
Like um when I looked out there when I was there she was down there on the ah the river.
What river?
Our river, the Grafton.
When did you see the Grafton River, the Clarence?
The Clarence in Yamba anyway it is all there and I can't get it.
You cannot visit?
No.
You can't visit with your family or anything?

Thank you very much for coming.
You are most welcome.
[Silence]
What were you thinking just then?
I was thinking listing to the noise out there and remembering I really had a lot of I didn't realise this till sometime this room was here for somebody to come into it and I was um here a bit but not I had to have a place where I could um look after to be looked after and I didn't realise that it was what it was I don't know.
Do you think you got put her because of your dementia?
Oh no that was way back. I think it was the... what that it's a bad thing I spent a fair bit of time... um that cancer thing.
The melanoma you had on your back.
Yeah.

84

What about it?

Well I think that's down the way down that's where I had with that anyway ... Jenny

The Jenny who works here?

Ah no um RC what's her name?

RC

Yeah she was telling me about the the um child the mother has that is very out of it but being very um amazing with what she can do um and she does a lot of working with her hands and um she can't do ordinary school or anything like that.

Who is this?

R's has a sister who has this stuff that she can't work with. She goes to school and she was telling me how she could wants to do something with language.

Sign language?

Yes.

Some people are amazing.

What is nice about lying down on the bed?

You are safe. You hear things.

So you like to pray and reflect while you are lying on the bed?

The dementia has really knocked me out altogether. I don't know I um love music but I I've got some beautiful songs but what I would really like is to have someone who would tell me and I'm not able that is what I am thinking.

You are not able to pray? You are not able to reflect?

Yes. I don't know how to say things 'cause I can't ...

Find the words?

Yes ... well think for nice things I am surprised that um the people who have to do the um they never speak to me but of course that would be the same with anybody and I'll live but it has been an awful waste.

What's a waste?

Well I can't do things.

So you are saying that your life is a waste?

Could be.

Wow! I'm gonna smack you with my walking stick.

What?

I'm gonna smack you with my walking stick.

Why?

For saying that your life could be a waste. Just because you are unwell does not mean that your life is a waste.

... get things from the river.

Stones?

Water. You know you can talk you can with people like that if you want to make...

Sorry Mary I hate to have to say this but I am not following you on this one. I am not sure what you are trying to say.

That is all right. There are too many things that I can't do that I would like to and I can't.

What would you like to do if you could?

I'd like to go out and see people. I'd like to get information on the river on what they're doing. I'd like to think something nice before I let you go.

Winning lotto.

Money is no problem at all.

It isn't for some.

That's right. That's right.

Do they put the sides of your bed up?

No I don't like it.

Why is that?

I feel...

Hemmed in?

No.

Do you get bored Mary?

I don't think so. There is always something happening and when I decide I am going to do something um when you leave I'll go and see what is going on in the world and when I've done that I there are things that...

Keep your mind busy?

Yeah. And um I having this feeling I have isn't it nice to have a friend like that and I suppose it is because I was a child brought up very um we were very together and I think of things that I have like when after I was born Granny was wonderful person in our house. Grandfather was a nice man. He used to play the cricket and dad was a lovely man. I our house was always there was a couple I experiences when mum gave me a smack a really good one. The family that lived next to us that those people were also Irish people were getting out of England the part where Australia came from.

What part of Ireland did your father come from?

Let me get it... Tipperary down in the low go down go... Is there V- V-...

Virgin?

No. They had don't know um... E's a very unusual name... Vikings! Vikings!

Yeeha! [Mary yells in delight] Yeeha Mary! Do you know where the Vikings come from?
Europe. Norway I think.
Yeah. She thinks her ancestors were from the Vikings.
B?
Um … not us they're different people but they are not talking the same not talking about Australian the …
The family history can be traced back to the Vikings?
Yes!

I feel sorry for her. It is very difficult.

Mary is commenting on one of the severely demented clients who just walked into and then out of her room.

Do you think you would be like that one day?
Yeah.
How do you feel about that?
Oh well if it really is like that um I'll have to handle it or the others will have to handle it. [Laughter] But the thing is that we are I am Australian and what happened for me in my very early life was amazing when I look back on it
You are an amazing person. Not were, are!

There is a lady who comes in on Tuesday's with what's called um music for a music for soothing …
Ah … meditative stuff?
Yeah and that this all of the …
Clients?
Yeah are there and very interesting.
Interesting how?
Well they're all sorts of people and I'm trying to do something with this and I can't.
Um …
You were talking about the music.
Yeah well it's interesting. I've come to sing songs when I've got to have it in front or I gotta see and get it going and it's just I'm liking it I'll sing you a song.

And she did, singing 'It's a long way to Tipperary'.

It is. I've been there and my hearts been in it. Um … there is a really nice one up in … sigh! See. I can't do it!

I start Mary off on another song, 'The Road to Gundagai'.

And it happens to be two songs that I find so uplifting. I went to Tipperary and Gundagai. Dad when he got and job when he came into Australia he got um and by this time my mum had she and and this... what is it... dad was from Ireland and he was an Irishman and he married my mother...
Funny thing!
She went when Dad went to work it was in put him down the ground to run through the country side...
Roads?
Roads. Mum must have been there a certain amount of time when dad went to that place they were young people so I like Gundagai.
So tell me, why is music so uplifting for you?
For me. I like when, makes me feel good. Especially ones I know also ones that give something.
Help you to remember things do they?
Yeah.
So when you sing about Tipperary you remember the memories and feelings you had when you were in Tipperary. The same with the stories your mum and dad told you about Gundagai and the memories make you feel good?
Yes.
So you can remember things when you sing those songs?
Yep.

4th July 2015

It was during this visit that I noticed that Mary has begun smudging her words. That is not quite the right way of describing it. It is a bit like someone pressing the on/off button on a tape and what you hear are cut off versions of the word, but not enough to understand.

I'm worried that Jenny's dead.
You're worried that Jenny is dead - Jenny from Kempsey?
Yeah.
The one that comes up nearly every month?
Yep.
You are worried that she is dead?
Yes.
Oh! Who do you think I am?
Ah! I shouldn't have said it I just...
Jenny who does all the photos and who drew the picture of the hands for you?
Yeah.
You think she might be dead?
Yeah and I can't find her... not her them... I don't... I don't want to go into... I probably do it...
Can I say I'm the healthiest looking dead person that you've seen!
[Laughter]
No wait a minute...

Who the hell do you think I am?
Oh, I've made a mistake.
[Laughter]
It is good to see you Mary. Thanks for amusing me.
[Laughter]
Well that was funny.
Well I'm glad…
So what's my name … my last name?
Jenny is um um … I can't get it.
Clarke
Yeah I should have got that.

This is a beautiful blanket. Where did you get it from?
Um somebody. No Jenny here. No somebody here gave it to me and it wasn't one of the people it was somebody in the it wasn't one of the names like it was somebody in where where where! I am you know where I anyone know they gave they wouldn't be using it so I took it. I felt got back to Jenny um I give her that laugh laugh …

You're Jenny Clarke. The other Jenny who?
I'm Jenny Clarke I am from where?
I think it is from Kempsey.
Yep you got it right.
What about the other Jenny?
There is another Jenny, not Clarke, who works here. I do not know what her last name is.

How is your sister and the baby?
You mean my brother and the baby?
Yes.
G. is seven now and doing well. My sister R. said to say hello to you and so did my sister K.

So you are feeling unwell Mary?
No. Um I think I there is something wrong. Um I actually before you came I um … um … ta … I put in um words rather than … um somebody um … I know there is something wrong with me and I write a little thing to say to the lady who is supposed to care for me not in the convent but there person in the place I'm in … what's the place I'm in?
St Michaels.

St Michaels. Um I think when I get what I wrote I'll see to you and see what happens. There is something wrong with me. I think it's um … I think, well I know I feel terrible and I think it because I'm a nobody in that area. I think she well I think she's no no well I was was going to say that she has no idea of me um it's the thing that I don't know. She doesn't do anything for me.

What does it feel like saying that you are a 'nobody' or that you feel you are a 'nobody'?

Hum! Um! I ah can't do anything. I'm a nobody …

You feel powerless?

Yeah. That's the thing powerless. What I am going to try to do is I haven't had any um I'm not there …

Mentally?

I think so. I don't make any … and I thoughted I'm just, I'm … I'm a nobody

And you just thought that?

There are people here that the girls work there a number of them and some of them are really really good friends but I think that the I have no way of knowing things getting near things my, my, my friends my um my um … find the nuns. There are other people … I'm in a mess and I'm thinking of saying to finding one in the place to whom I can say I want to go for a holiday. But I don't think I will get one. Or to talk to somebody but I won't get it I don't think but anyway, wanyway. There is God and a few other people. I'll be right but I'm bad …

Now you are saying that you are a 'nobody'. If you were seen to be a 'somebody', what would you do? If you had power, what would you do?

I'd um meet people. Um who recognised me. I don't want them to do anything for me but to be recognised as somebody. Does that make any sense?

It makes so much sense Mary that it has reduced me to tears … Mary Magdalene Quinn, I recognise you as my friend.

I know that.

I recognise you as one of the most brilliant women I have ever met in my life. I recognise you as a woman who has made an immense difference for me in my life. Always will, no matter how unwell you are … I recognise you!

Thank you.

I thank you. I'll just tell you this little thing. I was trying to think out my friends and my people who are mine in my who I am in Mary Quinn. No what was … I talked about the man one of our our ladies who were married recently in Ireland. Did I tell you that … I've lost it … Oh yeah! A couple of days ago I remember the blast the remembered that the song I love best and it is a Irish sing. I must tell you it but I can't get to it. Um I remember but not straight on the spot.

Why were you on the bed when I got here? You said you were unwell. Was that physically or was that because you were sad?
Not so sad. Grrr! Something hit me in the head there. [Pointed to jaw] It was something in my head and sore like somebody hit me.
And you got a headache?
No. It was though somebody threw something at me.
It was like somebody hit you in the side of the head?
Um!
And it hurt?
Truly but anyway the lady got onto and by the time you came along it worked off.
You seemed really sad when I got here?
Hum! Yeah that is what is part of what I've got on my head. Will I do it or will I won't I do it.
What would you do?
Drop it because I think it is gone but anyway...

I'm just going to remove all this chocolate. It is very hard to eat delicately at that angle. Don't worry.
I have to do it as I cannot talk seriously with you when you've got chocolate all over you face. You look like an idiot!
[Laughter]
Ain't I a lovely friend!
[Laughter]

Um I'll go back to Ireland singing.
What are you going to sing?
I'm going to tell you what it is. I tell told it was song that I remembered was my favourite song. Did I ever do that?
You told me that you had a favourite song but you haven't told me what it is yet.
It's um.... it's I think it is down there I heard it it sing when I was in Ireland when I worked in the nuns and I think I snag it after when I came over here and then I forgot it all and then then and not just be just a couple um short time here um it came back to me and that was really nice. The song itself is is one of their things over there for themselves it was so good. I think it was

92

down in in down in the Ireland in the corner of … what's that place?
Tipperary?
Yes Tipperary and I'm going to get someone to get it back to me. It is a lovely lovely thing. I think it is one of their that family is good around the people there. I don't know if that is true though. I think it is so. It is something about um the water going out um in the land and coming back and it is really lovely song.

I started to sing Danny boy and we both sang a few lines together then we laughed.

No it is not that one anyway that.
I think I know the one you are talking about but for the life of me I cannot remember it either I'm sorry.
That is all right. Okay.

Give me some advice.
About?
Will I do you think I'll get anything from trying to get over things in this place just take it it is there.
Do you think you will get over it?
Yeah?
You do not get over what you've got. You just gradually get worse. You always told me that I had to be honest with you and I cannot tell you anything but the truth. You've got dementia.
That actually doesn't bother me now.
It doesn't?
No but the fact that the lady in that place whose runner is what I … anyway.
So, if having dementia doesn't worry you anymore why were you so sad this morning when I came in?
[Silence]
Let me put it another way, is it because you've got dementia that you think that people think you are a nobody?
No it's um that I can't do.
Can I take that one step more, can't do what?
Um to see my um my sisters in the convent and my own sisters.
So you think that you are a nobody because you cannot do anything out there in the world? Let me ask it in another way when you were well and you could travel all over the world and you were working and you saw people in nursing homes and looking at how fragile and frail they were. Did you feel as if they were nobodies? That they had nothing to offer when

you visited the sisters in St Catherine's and places like that. You still cared for them. You still thought that they were somebody. So, why don't you give yourself the same consideration? You're in a nursing home now. It is your turn because you are unwell, you're aging and fragile. Don't you think you've earned the rest and the respect of the rest of humanity? One day we are all going to be in your position. We might not all get dementia or be in nursing homes but we will become unwell and frail. It takes a lot of courage to get old and to be old.

Thank you.

Thank you that it has made you think of it in a bit of a different way?

Yeees!

Do I have to smack you every time I come in to reteach you this lesson or throw a piece of chalk at you?

[Laughter]

I think that what I get is what I've already got.

Well that's profound!

Huh?

I don't understand. 'I think I've got what I've already got'?

Well what I'm thinking is I can't get and it is not anybody's it's not those people that are there, there are things that I can't get 'cause I can't get but there are people behind that and they are making things let go.

I am trying to understand this. You mean there are things that you cannot get mentally? You don't understand things? Is this what you are trying to say?

That's not you know a lot of the people I do like the things that I can do they're things that are there and instead of doing things be happy with that [Mary makes a frustrated noise] is what I should get rid of. There is a lot that I get but I miss what I don't get. I better get myself together and get on with it. I've got you and I've got people in the … even if I don't get the person who gives no money to me that I expect should do me.

Do you need money?

Me?

Yeah?

What do I want money for?

Exactly so why are you talking about money?

That's not about money.

Oh okay!

I'm not talking money.

Right …

I want ability.

You want ability. So you wish you had the ability to do things?

Nooooo…things like I can't um go to the I can't go to my sister she lives along railway in the area and when she gets um knowledge and I could go down um I don't know. It's its…

You want the physical ability to be able to do things and get out of here?

No I want to see things. I would like to um ladies you said somebody and who did you the thing to you put somewhere?

You mean the Mercy cross?

Yes. What is it?

The Mercy cross I took the photo of in Grafton?

And what did you do?

I put it on the wall here in your bedroom.

Oh she was one here down near there somewhat okay. Pray for me. I'm staying here today not going back over there I'm…and I'm going to see if I'll do what I can do and leave the rest alone. Do you think that good idea?

See what you can do and leave the rest alone?

Hum!

You mean accept your illness?

NO! [Shouted] What I cannot do.

We've all got to accept what we cannot do. That is what loss is about isn't it?

Yes!

Loss is an echo of what once was.

[Silence]

What are you thinking?

Thinking of those things then and the things that are there and they are beautiful but I can't put my hand out and touch them.

Mary talking about the flowers in her room.

Do you want me to bring them close to you?

No no other things that are there also…

Are you ticklish?

Hey?

Are you ticklish?

Nooo!

You sure?

Yeees. Why?

I could see if you're ticklish!
[Laughter]
Try. See. I'm a useless person.
Why do you say that you are a useless person?
Because you don't get tickles out of me.
Well I could do it to your feet.
[Laughter]
Why do you think you are useless not being ticklish? I think it is a good skill not being ticklish.
Makes bad tickles.
My nephew is very ticklish. He gets nervous when I ask him for a hug 'cause he doesn't know if I am going tickle the hell out of him or give him a hug.
[Laughter]

Well will I continue to what did I say I wanted to do - run singing up the middle of main street.
What!
[Laughter]
I um I'm going to say, ask for some um something that I don't get um because I'm out of place. That doesn't make any sense to you!
I think having dementia would make anyone feel out of place.
Yeah! What is it actually?
Dementia?
Yes.
It is a decline in your brain's ability to think and reason and remember. Over time it gets worse and then it starts to affect your functional capacity and your ability to communicate with others. Hello is anybody home?
No!
[Laughter]
And the good thing is you've still got your sense of humour. And it makes you forget people. For example, when I first got here this morning you were telling me that your friend Jenny was dead.
Yeah.
That was me.
Yeah.
That was because your mind wasn't thinking right. It took a while for you to realise that I was the Jenny that you were talking about. Maybe that is because you haven't got your glasses on and you couldn't see me real well.
[Laughter]
So, why did you ask me what is dementia?

96

Um! I don't…I can't put it in me head that I'm believing that I do something silly. I'm a I can't make, I can't make it up but I'm still the same.
You are still Mary Quinn…
Oh yes!
…you've just lost a number of your memories. It does not make you any less the person you are.
[Sigh]

I'll see what I can…yeah! I'll wipe that little piece of writing.
You don't remember how to write though.
I do! What?
I don't think so.
Okay. How did you get out of it?
How did I get out of what?
[Mary is sounding agitated]
Well you are one of the millions of people who don't get dementia.
Oh! But I might get dementia.
Yes you might but you haven't got it.
Not at the moment no. Does that make you angry that I don't have dementia and you do?
A bit.
A bit! Yeah. Your mood just changed. You sound really cranky at the moment.
What! I was just putting that in but I'm not well I didn't think I was de…
Cranky!
Yeah! About it because I know it's no it's something that you can't think co to say ys don't do it you don't do it.
The thing is even if I don't have dementia it is not going to make you feel any better about you having dementia!
Okay. We'll let you go home.
You are going to let me go home are you?
[Laugh]
You want me to leave do you?
No!
I thought that you were angry with me.
I'm a long is yeah. Can you hear the mm the mi the singing in the…
There is an Irish bloke out there singing now.

Okay let me ask you are very serious question.
Okay let me get se…serious.

Did you just say let me get serious?
Yeah.
[Laughter]
Okay. What would you like people to remember you for? When you eventually get called home by God in the future, how would you like people to remember you?
That I was kind. That I gave my my giving um was um um um what was good for the person being given... I um I don't think I ah well I can say that much. Giving. Like me be look out as a giving person. Loving makes me a bit 'ohowohwo'

I see you as a loving person. What does 'ohowohwo' mean?
[Laughter]
I said something about giving that is what I think is my biggest thing is giving. But you can't always give if you haven't got it.
You have given most of your life. Sometimes you get to a point where you can no longer give because you are unable to give because you are unwell.
Mm-hmm!
And that is where you are at the moment.
Yeah.
But I see you as still giving in that you are sitting here talking to me. You will still give me your friendship.
Yeah!

We were listening to Val Doonican singing. I had told Mary that he had died the day before.

Well he is lucky.
That he has gone to God?
Mm-hmm!
Would you like to go to God?
Yep!
You would like?
Yeah oh no that is not the way to put it. God is always there.
Are you sick of struggling of being the way you are?
How do you mean? In what way?
Frustrated at not being able to get a sentence out at times? Not being able to look after yourself?
Well there are a number of sisters over there can you see where te op te li are
M.H.?
No they're with me. There is a group here out in the middle they're in

they're ... [Mary snarls] I better get out of it ge ol fe ...
Are you feeling cranky with them?
No. I'm a in that area there are not a a inside oui th I part of something ... I don't know. I might try and find one of these days ... is this yours? That's good.
Why would you be wearing something that belonged to me?
[Laughter]

Did you know Sr Mary I think she is was old lady she is still alive in Sydney.
No, I don't think I do Mary.
Yeah! Is St Michael's a big place?
I don't know how big the place is. At least 100 beds I would say. It has got upstairs too, but you are on the ground floor.
Yeah.

What are you looking at?
Just there just down there.
The grass?
Yeah!

My friend Mary! My beautiful friend Mary.
My friend ...
Jen ...
Jen and she is still alive.
[Laughter]
By gosh that was funny. I've never seriously had someone tell me so seriously that I was dead. I hope you are not doing a Nostradamus and giving me a premonition.
What is that?
Nostradamus is that really old bloke from several centuries ago who has made some startling predictions about humanity. Said that the third world war would be fought along religious lines. Anyway what I was saying that I hoped your words about me being dead was not a prediction. I don't think I'm going to go any time soon besides I made a promise that I would wait until you went first to pave the way for me.
[Laughter]
Make sure that they all know that you're coming 'cause they all better run and hide.
[Laughter]

What did you say about this thing that it was what?

What thing?
This thing down here, here no here.
The TV?
NO here! There are three things there and you are sitting on the end.
You mean these photos? And the drawing I've done?
Yeah!
That is the drawing I've done oh about 12 months ago of our hands. I outlined my hand and I outlined your hand.
Yeah that's right.
And that is the photo of the Macleay River and that one is up-river on Willi Willi Road.

What are you thinking?
Thinking about you.
Mm-hmm! And what a problem child I was to teach?
No you weren't.
I wasn't? Oh I hated school. Funny isn't it.
It is.

We started talking about sisters in Kempsey.

You want me to go and see M.? I haven't seen her as I was told that she was fully into dementia. I didn't want to disturb her. Having two disturbed people in the same room would be enough I'd reckon.
[Laughter]
What does she do?
Who M.?
Mm-hmm!
I have no idea. She's in the same predicament as you are. She has dementia too.
Yeah.
So she wouldn't be able to do anything.
Well thank you!
[I believe that was said ironically]
Snort! I didn't know you did …
[Uncontrolled laughter]
Oh God! I really put my foot into that didn't I!
[Laughter]
Ah ha!
[Laughter]
I hp dii un di out there have we had bread ad libed …

Lunch?
Lunch?
No!

Now can I rephrase what I just put my foot into?
Yees!
Okay. The reason why M. can't do anything because she is completely demented–in that she does not know anything. She does not know how to look after herself anymore. She has lost her memory of everything.
Yeah...
M. cannot do anything for herself any more, like you know you are having difficulties doing anything. Like you cannot shower yourself anymore. You need help with physical activities etc.
Yeah yeah.
She often sits there and stares into space.
Is that what I do?
It is what you are coming to. How does that make you feel?
Aw golly, I don't want people washing me.
Washing?
Yeah.
But that happens now Mary. Don't the nurses help you with having a shower?
Yes. Yes it is not always...

Has the pain gone from your face?
Yes. Don't know what did it. It went through there [Mary pointed] like somebody hit me there and then it went into there and that oh...what am I going to do.
When that happens again you call the nurses immediately.
Why?
Because it could be heart pain.
Oh!
It is possible your heart is playing up Mary.
Yeah.
How does that make you feel?
No no. I know that I've got people who are good after those things and the nurse came immediately. One thing which came from dementia is...somebody does washes me and I don't know it.
You mean you forget?
[Silence]

101

I love you Mary.
I love you too. I know all the wonderful companionship we have had ... that's the um where are we there? Do you know where it is?
Where what is Mary? It is a blanket. A beautiful blanket. A blanket that I might pinch as I am leaving.
[Laughter]
Soft ... there are some things up here I wa so uh some of the some of the what is it ... the material is just so soft.

Does the thought of dying scare you Mary?
Nope. Nope are you?
Um, no I don't think so. I go to counselling because sometimes I get really angry with my pain and stuff like that. I thought that I needed some counselling to balance myself out. I get sick of the physical struggle sometimes.

What are you thinking?
I'm looking at the the there ... a lot of those things have been knocked out of my life.
A lot of what things?
What you just spoke on.
Mary are you referring to the plaque on your wall that says: "Mercy the principal path mapped out by Jesus Christ for those who desire to follow him." [Quotations from the Writings of Catherine McAuley. Page 297]
Yeah.
But aren't you still following him now in your illness?
I don't even think of it. I know it is dreadful.
Why is it dreadful that you do not think of Mercy?
Well I'm it some of the nothings I've got ...
You've got a lot of something to me.
I think the only thing I have is God is good.
You sound so depressed Sr Mary Magdalene Quinn that I feel like ...
[Laughter]
Don't you dare!
Thank God the woman is alive.
And wants to be!
Good. Excellent. But you still feel like a nobody?
[Silence]

I'm really enjoying sitting here enjoying the silence and the love that we

share. I feel so good just sitting here with you. Don't have to talk. Don't have to do anything. It's just really nice to sit here and be in your company. Thank you.
I love that.
And I love that you come.

Can you sing the first line?

So, I sang the chorus of 'When Irish Eyes are Smiling' and Mary joined in. It wasn't pretty, but it was enjoyable.

You do um you do much more. You know a lot of things that I don't know I know um I do. Do you know that?
I'm not sure what you are trying to ask Mary?
There are a lot of things that um … suddenly I hear. Who is that fellow is?
Val Doonican.
You've got that. I've got nothing like that to know.
Um you mean that I am pretty good at remembering things.
Yes Mm-hmm. Or picking up the good stuff in the minute, the fact that you picked them up. I don't know many things like that haven't got a lot of …
How does that make you feel?
Oh [sigh] Okay.
You don't sound okay
[Laughter]
[Mary makes a cranky sound in jest]
Exactly.
No. No I think it is wonderful that you are like that.
It is funny about humanity. We often do not think as well of ourselves as what other people think of us.
Mm-hmm!
And you are the same especially when you say something like 'you are nothing'.
I probably because you have moved around more.
You've travelled all over the world. I haven't.
[Laughter]
You've gone to a lot more places than I'll ever hope to get to Mary Magdalene Quinn!
[Laughter]

I know your brother don't I?
Yes, D.

He worked in the jail at some time didn't he?
He did!
Wow! I knew something.
Yes.
[Laughter]
You did. Well done. I remember last time I was here you were trying to remember the word Vikings, but you came out with virgin instead. We laughed about that and then you remembered Vikings. You were so excited and you yelled out Yes! Yes! Yes! Did we laugh! Do you remember that?
Yes I do.
It is an amazing skill to remember something. You've got 80 odd years of filing up there and I've only got 57 years, so it has to be a lot harder for you to find things than it is for me. There are a lot of things I don't remember.

I must get that song. I think I might have a sleep after lunch.
Oh what a good idea.

Do you want KFC tomorrow?
Yes please.
Okay, I'll bring some in.
Last time you came here it was beautiful. Yum, yum, yum.
[Laughter]
I'll remember that. Can I have some yum, yum, yum please. I personally think that it is good to have some take away food occasionally.

Okay my love, my Irish eyes, I will see you tomorrow
Thank you and I won't make a fuss.
Yes you will if you get that pain in the jaw again. You need to let them know.

5th July 2015

Don't mind.
Nope. I don't mind at all.
Ah. What would want you to come to here this morning?
I come every Sunday morning that I am up here.
Do you?
Every 4–6 weeks depending on how things are going with me. Okay put this in your hand. I cannot put it there until you get the stunned mullet look off your face. Mary who am I?
You don't think I don't know!
[Laughter]
I think you do know but I think it is very hard in finding a way outta ya brain.
Well I don't think I've been in here.
Ah ha! I think your 'demuntia' is playing up today.
Why?
Because you are in your bedroom and that I come and see you ever 4 -6 weeks and I've done so for the last 18 months to 2 years in this nursing home.
Yeah! I didn't think I had in here I don't know anyway. Forget it. I am interested in the Irishman that we spent some time on yesterday. Did I?
I just told you that an Irish singer Val Doonican died. He was 88.
Has he just died?
He died on Friday morning I think.

He started with Irish eyes and my favourite one out of the Irish is it looks like it is the last one. It is an interesting song which is I think it's in the ah where the ah down down south where the water came in from the … that's not probably right that is what happens and it is a beautiful song. It is my favourite.

I wish I knew which one it was so I could sing it to you but I don't know it.

So, what was it about Katarina that made you so angry when she reached across you?

Because she, they get into my clothes and put them there and scratch me and go on. I want my own life!

You want your own life! Yeah. Did you realise you had a lot of butter on your sleeve?

[Mary is sounding agitated]

No!

So you don't like people in your personal space. That is good to know. So you don't want me to give you a hug anymore?

There are good people. There are people who know me.

Yeah right. So it is okay for me to do it.

What is the name of the … the name of the … Oh! I can't get the words in the right place so I'll leave it.

What's the name of the song?

No, what you ate?

A wagon wheel.

Yes that is it wagon wheel. I hate being, I don't know the places next to us in getting where you go where you are going to where ever it is being knocked out of Grafton is a big 'scruches' me.

It made you very angry?

Yes.

So the process that you don't like is developing dementia and being sent from Grafton to St Michaels. You would rather have been given another choice?

[Ironic laughter] What could you do to … I don't know … They don't know!

They don't know what?

They just take the thing boom she's here.

They didn't even give you a choice?

No.

[Mary is sounding very agitated]

They just moved you over without telling you.

That's right. That's right.

And that makes you angry?
Mm-hmm.
What made you think of that now?
Now?
Yeah. Did the mint slice give you indigestion or something?
[Laughter]
No. I just feel not wanted.
You feel not wanted.
Or cared for... there have been beautiful people in here but they don't get
don't get
th...
What can we do to make you feel wanted and cared for?
Say that again.
What can we do to make you feel wanted and cared for?
I don't know.
It is a hard one isn't it?
It is.
Do you believe that you are wanted and cared for by me?
Say that again.
Do you feel wanted and cared for by me?
Yes. I I highly ah grats I ah um you are just so wonderful really.
But you do not feel as if many people are being there for you?
...no id...

*Yesterday you kept on saying that you felt like a nothing. Is that what you
are feeling again today?*
Ahm! Well I know it's thing I'm in and I can't get out of it. It is like being in jail.
It is like being in jail. The dementia is like being in jail?
Well it is not the dementia so much it's that people can't get me it's what they
can do with it I mean I anyway we'll leave it alone kl now. You know that well
don't you that there that lump iss place here do you? If I could um um... you
see out there is sitting here in Grafton really.
You feel that being out there is like being free...
Yes...
... having freedom
Yes.
And being in here is like being in jail?
Mm-hmm! And I'm ah I'm worried about this lady that she never speaks to
me.
Which lady are we talking about now?

107

The person the she is another person I am talking about this part of the world in everybody's little world is in um what is it it's the one that is next to us me but I don't get anywhere to get that. I don't know! That piece of work there there where the chickens are, the next place that goes out goes into where I'm supposed to be being looked after and that goes it all goes out there. It is such a wonderful place. It's a bugger. There are a few things that come past and I wonder um I could get a bit of that's nice... I don't know. I am a baby I suppose.

You are a baby. Is that what you just said?

Yeah.

Eh! Cutest looking baby I've ever seen!

[Laughter]

At least I made you smile.

You go on with what you were going to say.

I have no idea I cannot remember.

Well I um just my I s wi 'ahahahah' I over on the other side the mass the mass one of the things I can do is I see other people can do worse than I do and I went to it wasn't a mass it was...

Communion?

...communion and she um I came in to the church and said hello to one of the girls and the girls and the...

H. sisters?

Yes the H. sisters. I said hello to her and got down and she got and said I better go and see if D. I better see, she is not here. She is in heaven. It is such an agony for that woman and things like that touch me and that is nice so I'm not being 'angwangyanny' all the time.

So you really feel for K.'s pain?

Oh yes. It's not...

I don't think you could be accused of being a cranky old thing all the time. Is that what you think people think?

What?

I don't think you could be accused of being a cranky old thing all the time. Is that what you think people think?

No!

Good! I'm so pleased 'cause you are not a cranky old thing all of the time— only 90% of the time.

[Laughter]

Sorry. I had to throw that one in there. I couldn't help myself.

Oh dear. No... I wish I could walk. What are you chuckling at?

The image of you in a snit walking. It would be a sight to behold. You would probably thump me if you could walk after me stirring the hell out of you all the time. Or pick up something and throw it.

[Laughter]

Don't say that again.

Yes mam. So why would you like to walk? What difference would it make if you could walk?

Oh well it's the one thing in there that the H's no its not that its me me the Sisters of Mercy they can the ones that can walk out of that they go I could go down the road. Yes go down there and meet on of the kids girls from here and have a lovely afternoon.

You feel more of a prisoner because of the fact that you cannot walk at all...

Oh right yes.

... as you do with your dementia?

Yes.

That is a reasonable thing. I know that I sometimes feel a prisoner because of my disability. So yes, I sort of understand. You are a prisoner in two ways: in your mind and in your body. I think the reasonable thing to do here would be to shoot you and put you out of your misery.

[Laughter]

That is what we would do to our horses at home. Oh, you're gonna hit me now, aren't ya? Nope.

There is a knock at the door and Mary's sister P. walks in. Mary is absolutely delighted to see her. She claps her hands together in joy.

8th August 2015

Mary no longer remembers my name and it does not appear to ring a bell when she is told what it is. She does remember that she knows me although it took a while for us to develop a connection at this visit.

You are so good. You know me. You do not want me to do anything now. [Mary sounds distressed]
Mary you are my friend. Just because you are losing your mind doesn't mean I am gonna lose my mate!
[Laughter, Mary aims a fist at me with a smile]
See this, if you know anything about it. A lady died yesterday.
A nun?
No ... she was a girl that I had some wo ... kids and something she was in the higher level in where they lived ... where is the last of the places up here?
Where are we? In Grafton or Casino?
No further st ...
Lismore?
Right up.
Brisbane?
Yes and beyond from that. She had children and um there was some connection that I cannot get it into my head but obviously you do know what she was about. She she she was a sick young woman.
Cancer?

I don't think she was sick. I want to get out of her name.
Mary I cannot help you with that one. I do not know your friends up there.
Yeah that's right.
Sorry.
That's okay. There was something that I wanted to say? Would you like to go somewhere with me this time? No cost to you.
Like where are you thinking?
Well um are they could go to the go to the uuuuuuum over here where the I realise what takes a long time for me to say things in this reason …
Did you say that it takes a long time for you to say things because of your dementia?
Yes. Well it is not the dementia it is me. I can't well that is the same thing um um we got a big water hole down near Grafton. What do people do with that?
What do they do with the water?
Yes.
Well they swim in it, drink it.
No they do things with it in the places that put people over that put water in it. [Laugh] You see that is how mad I am. Anyway that's that.
Are you talking about a water feature of some kind?
No. No. No! Get water put it out there put it in.
Dams?
No I better get out of it.
You want to go back to somewhere else. How can we do that with you who can hardly walk and me just as bad? How would I get you in the car?
We wouldn't go in the car.
How would we go?
Wouldn't uh two people go in the car but not in the car.
I could drive you in the car Mary. Just getting you to and into the car is what I cannot do.

R. came over a few days ago.
Did she?!
Yeah and I was very pleased. I looked at her standing there and I said R., R! [Mary said this in an excited voice]
So you knew her straight away! Who am I?
[Laughter]
Ah I think her name is Mick.
What's my name?
[Laughter]

I think you're … I haven't got the words yet. Oh! Isn't this terrible. I've knocked it about. Um! Um!

Can you remember where I come from?
Yes north.
North? No I come from south.
Do you?
So if I told you I was from Coffs, would you believe me?
Yes I would.
What about Macksville?
Doubtful.
Port Macquarie?
So you haven't said the right one yet?
No. What if I said that you came from Kempsey?
Well I thought that firstly that's what was.
Well the truth is that I do come from Kempsey.
Well there you are.
Can you think of my name now?
Who said you didn't have a name?
I do have a name but do you know what it is?
[Laughter]
Ah! I know it but it won't get out of my head.
That's okay. Do you want me to tell you what it is?
No no. Oh you might as well. I'll think about what it is next time. What is it?
Jenny
Jenny. Jenny.
Now you are going to have to remember that 'cause I am going to ask you my name again in an hour.

What does it feel like to hug somebody you love?
It's just this thing that is happening is totally there is not a person telling me what to do … to put a person who comes into my mind by coming in me not knowing and someone looks at me and says who it is, I think it is the world.
So you were so excited to remember her name?
No not that. Yes to know her name. I didn't have any trouble looking at her and knowing her.
So how does it make you feel when you do not remember somebody's name?
Oh the first thing I realise is that I know that person and I've got to get to let that other person some oh um its where is that girl just like I did when I said

that I was in the northern part of the world ... I'm trying to get other words to put where she is. I can't put a name on it at the moment um ... if I got in a car and drove straight up, up, up, up, what part of the world would I in?
Well you'd probably be past Brisbane on the Sunshine Coast somewhere. I don't know that part of the world at all Mary so I cannot tell you much.

You know it is okay not to remember somebodies name. It is frustrating though. The fact that you remember that you know them and love them is what is really important. What do you think?
Yes. Yes. I think lady did something the same way ... not that one. Haven't got it.
I'd like to take you out somewhere.
Why?
[Silence]
I enjoy being with you here. Do we need to go anywhere else?
Yes.
Why?
That's right you can't go out.
I cannot physically take you out. But again I ask you knowing that even if I cannot take you out why do you want to take me out?
Well I I'm not able, no that's not right. I um I'd like to get out and I can't and it is not because I can't or whatever ...

What are you thinking?
Um one of the nuns has probably will not be able to get a name. She has a made an offer um to take people, me places ... a will. She is it for a job to be done ... for me to be doing something like ... oh she'd be my age.
Ancient!
[Laughter]
With friends like me you don't need enemies.

What are you thinking?
You've turned the tables on me. What am I thinking? Well we've been sitting here quietly for five or ten minutes. We haven't said a word. We've been nibbling on our biscuit and I was thinking geez I'm lucky.
Geez I'm what?
Geez I'm lucky. I can sit here next to a woman who is old enough to be my mother ... pretty close to being old enough to being my grandmother too ...
[Laughter]

… but who I call a mate.

Hmmm!

And we can sit here in companionable silence, reflective silence and feel comfortable that we do not have to make a noise. I feel good sitting next to you not having to say anything just being comfortable with your presence. That is what I was thinking and I think it is a really good place to be.

Yeah.

So what were you thinking?

Um, um, um I've talked and that is different. I mean um I'm so glad you've come.

What is it about me coming that you like?

It's um the sort of thing that I like to do. Just sit here and listen to something that is nice. Bigger thing that you have someone that you like sitting with you. Being able to talk to somebody that I know would never do anything that would put me off my throw. It certainly it's lovely to be here in your um …

To be with each other together?

Yeah. I'd really like to get somewhere. You know …

You've got a case of cabin fever have you?

Oh no, no but that I want to …

You've got this frustrated look on your face?

Yees!

You're frustrated?

Yes you know … when she comes back from somewhere, if I wanted to do something for me … to make me more … it's not that … probably things um your um ah your um … what you can't do that's not saying that ckuidn but it is not going with you …

What town was R. born in?

Um? She comes from um … can't get it straight off.

Maybe Kempsey?

Yes.

So who else was born in Kempsey that you know?

Um, what's her name? She was a bit of a a um about the wrong thing you know it has to be this it has to be that … I can see her face but I can't hear her name. Do you know?

Jennifer Clarke.

Your name.

Yeah.

Was it you we were talking about?

Who did you think we were talking about?

Oh. She was an nardly top top.
She was a what, what?
[Laughter]
An elderly cop top?
No. Younger.
[Laughter]

She was very was should be done, shouldn't be done.
So she was black and white?
Yep.
Definitely not me! You are not talking about B.N. are you?
B. died didn't she?
Yes, she did. Sometime last year. B. your cousin did the eulogy.
Yes she did. Do you know her?
Yes she lives with another sister who is sight impaired. Amazing challenge to be living without sight.
Yes.

Would you take me out oh for lunch or would that be too hard?
I don't think I could do it Mary.
That is okay.
That is why I bring you KFC every Sunday morning because I can't really take you out. I could get the girls to put you in the car and I could take you for a drive but not get you out of the car. We could go for a drive around.
No. No.

Why didn't you sleep well last night?
Why didn't I. Didn't I?
No. When I got here they had just put you on the bed. They said that you did not sleep at all and that you were agitated most of the night and also agitated first thing this morning.
I don't remember that.
You feeling tired?
Yes.

9th August 2015

I've never seen this.
You've never seen this chicken before?
No.
Mary Magdalene Quinn you are looking gorgeous this morning, but your brain has gone on holidays. You've had this boxed chicken before. It's called a snack box and I get it for you every Sunday that I am up here.
Mmmm.
You have no memory of that do you.
No.
I still love ya.

Oh dear! Is it true to say, I get true get I think things and they are true…
Maybe you are remembering a memory?
I took up this morning oh Lord! I can't do that and then I thought oh I'm singing the song. So I muck things up. No I don't. Things are mucking me up. Isn't that right?
Yes things do muck you up.
I think that's all this is um all not a nice… I can up ah glad to remember a long way back. You know that song I haven't heard for years.
So why are you glad to remember a long way back and not, say, this morning or yesterday?
They um ah reminds me that mum used to sing that…

The memory makes you feel better?
Yes. Excited ...

What did you do last night?
I stayed at my sister's place. I went to bed at 7.30pm and read for a while.
I get tired easily these days. What did you do last night?
I met someone that I never saaaaw ... this morning I thought that the singing
that mum came out on was um I was shocked ... Is this fluffy stick stuff?
That is your washer. The box is here.

These things happen like I don't know that what happened or something
else anyway um is that that my a bad thing? Not a bad bad thing not good
for me?
I'm not sure that I understand the question Mary. Why is what bad for you?
Not being able to remember things? Or being cranky or not sleeping?
Yees.
Yes to which one?
What was the question?
I don't know
[Laughter]
You sat there and you said why and said why is it a bad thing. I do not know
what the question is.
Well the question is why does why um um make able to make things about
me that I don't and um I do things that I shouldn't think or is um are ...
Are you frustrated that you cannot do things?
Mmmm. What's the [Mary clap's her hands] what's the um no good what's ...
The use of living?
[Mary gives me a 'what the hell are you talking about' look. Laughter]

Well ... I don't know where you got this thing from [Mary points to a blanket].
It is yours. You like using it.
I must have lost my vision. I have not seen that for a long time.
Every time I am here, it is here.
Oh!

What ya thinking about?
Yesterday evening not ausnein it was um went a lot into what we were going
to do and I was waiting to get over to bed and whatever and I was worrying
because I was thinking I wouldn't be able to do to get to bed and it was quite
silly because the same time I was getting worried that I would never do and

where I was going and I looked I'll be going to get myself into the bed long time and I said that's okay and I'll let it go and I was thinking that I was out in the blue moon and there was no problem at all. I had food in the afternoon and that was that.

Are your eyes hurting Mary?
They are at times. And I'm hoping that I get the I don't want to go to here to get it.
They are taking you to a specialist sometime this week.
Now there there on that piece on the eye.
It is the corner that is sore?
Yeah. Anyway it will come around. The fellow who is over in Grafton I think is the right must I think it is right I'd like to get him back but I'm never in Grafton.
Maybe you will never get back there. How does that make you feel?
Dreadful.
In what sense?
Well the that was a much different to this other place. I don't even know where here is.
You are in St. Michaels in Casino.
Yes but I do not know where St Michael's is.
It is on the back road between Casino and Grafton. I do not know the name of the road. I think this back road was made during one of the world wars. Is that so?
I don't know.

So you don't know where Casino is on the map?
[Head shake]
NSW?
Oh yes.
So you know where Grafton is. Casino is north of Grafton.
That's right.
Then you've got Lismore, Ballina, Byron Bay and Tweed Heads.
[Sigh]
That was a big sigh?
Oh I don't get what I want in many ways…
[Laughter]
Get that face off!
[Laughter]
That is about the most profound thing I have heard all day.

[Laughter]

I'm sorry. We've got to entertain ourselves somehow Mary.

[Laughter]

Yeah! Yeah!

I don't get what you want?

About where I'm being and where I'm what's happening for me.

Do you know why that is?

Why?

I think because of the dementia.

Um!

Do you remember that you have dementia?

Oh well. I'll be dead soon!

Is that what you said? You'll be dead soon?

Yes.

What makes you say that?

Well um I don't get any contact with the nuns that are in Casino. I hate it!

That you don't have the contact?

No I just hate it being there.

You never liked Casino?

Didn't know it.

Oh!

So what makes you think you are going to die soon?

No it's not that I seen it's um … I just don't get at things.

You don't understand things anymore?

No.

Does it distress you that the dementia is getting worse and you are finding it difficult …

No! Blow it! Can't you blow?

Yeah I can blow it. I can tell it where to go. Life is and God is good!

Yes. I don't see M Whats-her-name …

K. She is upstairs

Yup. I don't know how to get there to see her.

Does that distress you?

The lady in charge all the things that are set out about my demuntia, whatever it is. Ahm I just have to put tis so and so she did it she is doing it. Let it go. There is nothing going.

Life is as it is.

What is that?

Life is as it is and we cannot change it.

Mmmm. I think it is whatever it is happens is on the that that what that lady has to say is there is nothing for me.

You got me.

Pardon?

You got me.

The certainly have and these girls here are but the rest of it ... get nothing about it from where my family is ...

Last time I was here Pat P. came.

Yes.

The nurse just told me that Pat P. came with her children a couple of weeks ago.

Anyway, it's not a happy, it's not a happy for all the mowainn.

So do you think you are depressed?

[Mary nods her head]

You do.

I have a sister who lives down the south. I can't know exactly where she is it is where I was in the place where I had the thing up here [Melanoma on the back] and her husband has the same thing that I have got and um ... I don't know what I was saying that for ... I would like to make contact with the kids that were at the schools. Kids I was friends with ... who are they? Um ... I think they are the people who run the um ... I think they are the people who run the ... um, um you know down in the river you have to have something if you want to get any use of it you have to have people to go in there and the ones that go into the water are the ones the oh no.

Lifesavers?

No, no, no, no ah a family run it.

Caravan park type of thing?

No! [Said with frustration] Um! Van, Van. I don't know! I do know but I don't know.

Yeah you do know but you can't get access to the file.

The people the name ...

It won't come out of your brain?

[Sigh!] No. Um the ...

[Laughter]

... the um one of the people who are in it are now I don't know what they are doing being in water and teeth the um there was a fellow when I was young that um belonged to this there the I think the man is the one that gets his teeth ...

You can't get it out of your head and you cannot get it into it.

120

This must be very frustrating?
Oh yeah!
This is irritating trying to get things out of your brain?
It is. I would like it is not Bailey it is something … Baileys it's not the Baileys. The fellow who thinking of in my mind is a fellow I really liked um what do you go to when you go to get your teeth done?
Dentist.
The dentist. He is a dentist. He is still a dentist but he might be finished but he might be retired but he was a nice guy. I've decided that I am not going to a dentist I'll just keep the teeth I've got in me. They've got I've got.
You look like you've got more teeth than I have got.

I don't have a lot of friends.
What! Have all of your friends died?
No no one of my friends have died.
Well I happen to know that you have a heap of friends Mary Magdalene Quinn.
What did you say?
I said that you have a heap of friends.
But not dead ones.
[Loud laughter]
This one ain't dead. She is still kicking. Well, I am just wondering why you are saying that you have got no friends when I know for a fact that you have a heap a friends.

Okay, where are you?
I was thinking that sisters and the I not in a big way I don't know much thinking about it but someone told me that so and so gone to Ireland and in the world today there are it is the the um Irish the Irish were we were part was um very close to where Australia goes and there were two of the sisters today this just goes across to um to Ireland and having a quiet um not a great big rum.
They are having a bit of a holiday?
Yeah I thought I do that I went I had that time in Ireland but it wasn't fun but it was wonderful.
You mean you worked?
Yes um but I was it is very much you don't have you can get over there in the area where we lived. I thought I wouldn't know enough because I couldn't get things out of my head um … I'm sure I wouldn't go back. No I'm not sure. But it is very unlikely.

How does it make you feel at this point in your life being 82 and knowing that there are certain things that you will never do again ever? Does that make you sad?

No, no because we are Australian nuns. What we did in Australia they are doing their work and we are doing ours.

You really loved Ireland and you loved working over there.

I loved the fact that Dad was Irish um. It's a beautiful warm but it had terrible things when Dad was in the war.

Yes that would have been horrible.

Yes ... Dad came from the place on the fighting.

He was from Dublin?

Yes I think that and he had a friend and one of his a and a couple of his children are still alive in here that was Dad's friend and he um was on the fighting side, Dad wasn't and um ...

He died?

Yes but this is I find this interesting, his friends children are still alive here in Australia and here in Grafton.

You are joking?

Nope.

Isn't that amazing?

And um I think there are two of them that live over the other side of the water and the youngest one that is um out the other side of the water, water runs all the time over there.

You mean the Clarence River?

Yes the Clarence.

So she lives over in South Grafton?

I'd like to go somebody so gave me a question to sss eck ... I don't know if I ever told you but this family had one boy not only one but there was one boy I'll think of it in a minute. I'd like to get over there on the other side and I think I will get something to go back to. The boy um who was there in the school, Kevin K. Did you ever know that there was someone who wanted to marry me?

Yes, you've told me that story.

Well Kevin's Kevin K's K died but the young girl is still alive and I think that there are three of them alive. I think I'll manage to go over one day. I forget the girls name but she is a lovely lady.

There is going to come a time and probably not too far into the future where you will not be able to go anywhere because you will not be well enough. How does it feel to be at this end of your life?

Well for me the end of that what goes up when you get up you're gone um is heaven and surely God is not being funny about it he is not going to do that. When I die it's the big thing is we all will know who God is. That is the way I look at it. That is the way I look at it.

So you are looking forward to dying and finding out what God is really about?

No I wouldn't say it that way. I'd be for me I will know now who God is and um who it's like meeting somebody. It it what we can out of what we already can learned in the world I'll go into saying, 'that's Jesus over there'...

And there is Mary over there.

[Laughter]

Is that what you are saying?

Yeah, yeah and to have um there is a thing in me that is grow, grow, grow... [sigh]

Growing?

Growing is Jesus is there and I had just recently I hey, hey I haven't been talking to Jesus for a long time. I wonder what he is thinking of for me. I'm not going to see him but I'm very interested in God. God is what is what I know. There is um arrr something other than in Catholicity um that goes with wondering what God is not having to not having um things about Jesus but about all religions and what's the one anyway it doesn't matter what one it is but there is one that ah I for those two things in my life part of other ones is Jesus and God and I'm tameid I now want to look at how who is God and you get a little bit of it being in the convent being those things and...

Do you think that by going to heaven you will get more of your questions answered and that everything becomes clearer and that's exciting for you?

Yep! And a part of it is when I go to the rosary's, I don't go to the rosary's I go to the th ws somethings what God has. God, Jesus is son.

So in a sense you are really looking forward to dying?

No! I want I will die but it is not worrying me.

If you knew you were going to die tomorrow, would that worry you?

No. Ah two days ago a lady died and she is someone I know but I do not know where she comes from but I do know that she and I were friends. Um I think she was one of my I don't think she was one of my students I think she had connection. She was in the northern world. She was my age.

Ancient!

[Laughter]

Had was like you with a body that you can't make work right...

[Long silence]

I am sad that you won't get to see the book in its finality.
Why?
Because you will be otherwise occupied somewhere else. I will be taping our conversations until you go. I cannot publish it until it is finished. Well, you can see it up there. If you do not like it you can come and haunt me.
[Laughter]
Oh dear! I am so grateful for a friend like you.
And I say the same back at you Mary Magdalene Quinn. I'm so grateful that I have a mentor and a wise woman who is my friend.
[We hug]

I wish I could get out of this dementia.
What would you do if you could?
I'd be able to um know what I know and what I don't know.
Yep.
One of the things I think that I am going to try having the dementia is just really rotten.
Yep it is rotten.
And I do I a wonder sometimes who the hell put this up. Is there any use for it?
Not that I am aware of, except for putting a hole in our Gross Domestic Product.
I still have a brain. Do you know that?
Well in actual fact, I do know that and I know for a fact because when I got here this morning you were pretty foggy and I've been conversing with you for the last two odd hours. You've become a lot clearer within the last hour. I believe that this is because I have been conversing with you and asking you questions etc.
Mmmm!
At the moment you are really quite sharp, so yes I do know that you have got a brain!

And what I want to do with this lady who runs this place, I get so cranky about her. She has no time for me at all and I've been thinking for a long time to um get my um brain out to work get make to that woman to understand that I have a brain thank you and I don't want to be in your mucky little place [Mary sounds cranky]. I'm going somewhere else where I can have my brain and work again, not work again but have the brain working.
But you need to also realise that the reality is that your brain is not going to work very well for very much longer. How does that feel?
Well I'd ask the question why not very good?

With dementia you gradually get worse and worse, to the point where you don't know. You don't even know my name any more. You know that you know me well, but you don't know my name.

No.

Last time I was here you could remember my name. It took a while but you remembered it. This time, even with hints, you cannot remember.

No.

So, gradually you are getting worse. Your brain will probably not be working as well next time I am here. It will perhaps take longer for our conversations. Probably five minutes after I've left you will not remember this conversation.

19th September 2015

I found Mary unable to verbally articulate what she wants to say. I don't know if this is to do with the patch that she was commenced on for her pain. I found that it has been difficult to have a conversation with her. She had difficulty in answering any of my questions. This is the worst that I have seen her. She appears to find the whole process of verbalising exhausting. Although she didn't appear cranky, the questions were frustrating for her in that she couldn't even figure out how to start the sentence. When I was here last time she was much better. This is the least articulate that she has been.

Where are you now?
I'm sitting in a chair at St Michael's in Casino talking to my mate Mary Quinn.
Oh. That's nice.
Are you with me?
[Silence]
You recognised me when I walked in. You smiled and said hello. Do you know who I am?
And I said???
You didn't say anything you just said hello.
[Laughter]
Do you know who I am?
[Silence]

Do you know my name?
Now? Yes.
What is it?
You mean now do I skmiumdn na...
Do you know my name now?
Yes oh dear ohhhhhhh dear I don't know.
[Laughter]
And the worst thing is I have five... bad die eyes.
Bad eyes?
Yes. I think this is quite funny well not funny but I don't think I can see things and I don't pass by people without realising say hello how are you but isufn somewhere just now in a couple of times um that's one of the things that's putting me in actually I am very less um I don't I don't see things ru si di cxj by the that's what the doctor is about but it is true but I cannot understand it but I will accept it.
You don't understand it and the fact that you don't know my name.
I don't know your name.
But you know that you are my friend.
Yes definitely.
If I told you that I came from Kempsey, would that remind you what my name is?
Yes.
Can you remember now?
When did I remember?
You haven't remembered now for a couple of months.
[Silence]

Do you able to get to R.?
I haven't seen R. for ages.
You've seen her?
No not since last year.
We had a lovely time this time when one of them died. Who died? I don't know. Anyway I am not gonna get into that too much because um you know you are worrying about that and that and that goes there and that shouldn't and that wouldn't and we do and why don't we um and ua...
Has someone died recently?
Um no...

So if I was to say that you used to throw chalk at me in class would you remember my name?

[Laughter]

Yes. You'd be telling a lie.

Oh would I just?!

[Laughter]

I don't think so. My name is Jennifer Clarke.

Yes!

Does that sound right?

Yes.

Good. I'll ask you in ten minutes whether you remember it.

[Laughter]

So, how have you been Mary?

I've been good actually for myself um I um ssssseee R came and we had a talk up which was nice very nice um. She took up how I was feeling and that was good.

She took up how you were feeling … so how were you feeling?

Oh I have to wait and think to think about. It was the [unintelligible] … I've just come from the the people who are work work like for um um work um and what was like you know people keep now place Jenny Jenny Jenny no to local people who are not nuns or something like that this place is … Too what did I say about … pretty much like to people that you sitting down in um we places to get to we get people where they do work and um but the most strange group of people there are a group in … strange group of people what place are they in?

St Michael's?

Yes yes! I list there last night or the night before that I found that very strange.

Did you have trouble sleeping last night Mary?

No. Why?

You just look really tired.

I was because I was in the situation that I was in that place I couldn't get into it um and uh I thought that they were going to throw me out.

What! Onto the street?

Mmmm.

That would have been a bit rough.

Well the people who went off and I was there it was strange. Where was I you said?

St Michaels.

No it wasn't the place anyway. That's interesting because I have never heard that I thought that where they came from I thought I thought. They are not. Where do you come from where I go come from have gone now.

128

I drive from Kempsey. I normally drive to Lismore and stay with my sister but she is not here at the moment. This time I drove straight to Casino. I am staying in a motel this weekend while I come and visit you.
What's her name? She is a nun over in Grafton somewhere along the is track is Jenny and she and she is about the same age... um and she she um does ordinary things she does things [unintelligible] and then all things happen its not stuff that you have to do or whatever and that she grabs me out of that did she do that...
She dragged you out of the dementia?

We were disturbed by the nurse who gave the following report:

Nurse: Mary has a pain patch. She has had it for two weeks. She also had a TIA (transient ischaemic attack/mini stroke) and a very bad case of the flu just after your last visit. She did not move for a whole week. Mary doesn't walk anymore. We use the machine to move her about and she is now in a wheelchair. She also does not feed herself anymore and she doesn't know most of us anymore.

Really! So what is my name?

Don't know....um Jenny.
Yeah!
Yeah!
[Laughter]

Nurse: Mary sits in her room now most of the time because she cannot stand the noise in the rest of the unit. We got her some hymns on CD and we have been playing them. She sang along. She got very emotional.

Will they move her out of this unit as she gets heavier?

Nurse: Only if she agrees. She has to say yes otherwise she stays here.

Does she still wake up during the night?

Nurse: No she sleeps straight through.

So you can't walk anymore?
Who told you that?
The nurses.
Oh.

How does that make you feel?
[Silence]

I saw your mother and father.
You saw my mother and father?
Before they died of course and I think that is interesting when they and I am sure that you mother is angry at your father's views... I can see in them I remember very because my father was the Irishman... I'd like to get her going one day, get something...
You right?
You never know.
You don't know?
Yes yes I do know. I can see you.
You can see me ... with my flanny shirt on.
Yes.
Do you know who I am now?
Yes...
I'm letting go now. You've got the cup all to yourself now.
What?
What! You've got the cup.

Before you go have you ever told me that um a man ah young man who wanted me to marry him?
You told me about a young man back about when you were 16 who rode a horse well. He loved you and wanted to marry you, but he knew you were committed to religious life. The next time that you saw him he was sick in hospital, but you managed to have a conversation with him before he died.
Yes I was sorry that I didn't I mean that I will be interested to see if got into heaven.
It will be interesting to see if he got into heaven?
Mmmm.
That's supposing that you are going to get into heaven. You might have to go to purgatory for a while.
I didn't think of that!
[Laughter]
I do believe that you would go anywhere else. I think that you are in purgatory and hell now Mary.
You are not! You are not!
I'm not what? In purgatory and hell?
Yeah you know hell.

We are in hell. Don't you think we are in hell?
NO! No!
What are we in then?
Whatever we're in it's not hell what do you call it!!... I believe that ahm no one ...

So we were talking earlier about your boyfriend and you were wondering if he would go to heaven. We were talking about heaven, hell and purgatory and you were about to tell me what you believed.
Mmmm.
So what do you believe?
[Silence]
So heaven, hell and purgatory what do you believe in?
Um what does do mostly ah the church believes I might be wrong but I think that they are the ones say ...
That when you die and you are good, you go to heaven; when you haven't been baptised or you need work on some of the wrong things that you did you go to purgatory; and when you are an absolutely monster you go to hell. That's basically it. Yes?
Mmmm.
What do you believe?
[Silence]

Come on wake up!
[Garbled] ... I'm trying to wake up.
You're trying to wake up but you can't.
I think that when I come behind me and I come I will see God.
When you die, life flows out of you. And when you open your eyes again you will see God?
Yep.
That is a wonderful belief. Of all the people in the world that I know Mary Magdalene Quinn deserves to go to heaven.
[Laughter]
And you too!
Oh no! You know what I deserve and it doesn't have to be heaven but it has to have a comfortable bed that I can lie on in total painless joy.
[Laughter]
Here let me get those cake crumbs. It is very difficult to have an intelligent conversation with someone with cake crumbs all over her.
[Laughter]

131

That is wonderful.

So, you opened your eyes when you died and God is there. When do you think you are going to die?

Don't know. I have no real I've nothing that is against me. These things these lollies are the only thing I go for except Jesus.

Except Jesus? You go for the lollies. The lollies and Jesus are the only two things in your life that are worth living for?

[Laughter]

No oh no Mum and Dad, life family. I'm just again I was I had my what do you call it J. I don't know but anyway I didn't have get a pick up day before yesterday. There is something about that but I don't know...

Would you like to die now?

No. What for? Do you?

Sometimes it is hard but no.

It hurts you to come here?

Sometimes it is really hard but it doesn't make me want to die 'cause I am coming up to see my friend Mary and it brings me joy coming and spending time with you ... I am wondering if you are getting tired of living?

Um ... um cough being sick of having...

Not being able to say what you want to say?

[Unintelligible]

Sick of having dementia?

You don't have dem... dementia do you?

No, I don't have dementia. I have a bloody poor memory at times, but I do not have dementia.

Mmmm.

Does that make you cranky that I don't and you do?

No. I um something that I was talking about something down in the council rooms now let me think...

Disturbed by the nurse.

I've got nothing running me.

You've got nothing running you. So your brain is not working at all?

No.

How does that make you feel?

Hmmm?

How does that make you feel not having your brain run at all?

But I don't have any I don't have anybody got ni I don't know anyway...

[Silence]

What are you thinking?

Trying to fi... which way I'm going.

Trying to figure which way you are going. In what sense?

Just looking at I am I in my I not knocking pieces off me yet. I'm trying to pick it up. Anyway—God is good.

You are an amazing lady. Why is God good?

Why is God good!

[Silence]

What are you thinking?

I'm looking at you and you look like the cranky maths teacher I used to know in school.

[Laughter]

Well now you know what is going on now!

Yes I've made you cranky.

I hate these I hate these. I think I need to get one...

You want me to clean them?

There are really nice ones you can get. There a two kinds that one's no good... [Unintelligible words] Well we'll give up those things we cannot understand.

What can't we understand?

I can't understand. It is plain I can't find what's this on my...

Come forward and I'll put your glasses back on. Is that better?

Yes I can see better.

Now who am I?

Who are you?

Yeah?

Jenny ah she has a name that I can't think of it and she's a beautiful woman she just...

Do you remember about 10-12 years ago I asked you to become Mum's friend and help her during the last years of her life and help her feel comfortable with death?

Yes I remember that and your dad was around then too.

Yes Dad was alive then too, but he died nine years ago. Mum was scared of dying and anything I said to her did not seem to help, so I got you involved. You helped Mum die well.

I liked your dad very much. He was a bit of a wag.

He was a real dry country bloke, wasn't he?

Yes.

We all miss our mums and dads. I don't think that will ever stop.

Okay I won't throw you out. I'm too tired.
Were you thinking of throwing me out?
[Laugh]
Have I done something to offend thee sister?
No not at all. You wouldn't do anything wrong for me.
I don't know. There are some times when I can be very offensive. Not to you but to others. I tell ya, some people can make me so cranky that I want to yell at them.
[Laugh]

Are you praying?
No.
Why do you sit forward like that then?
Well I think I need to need to going home and having some silence.
You need to have some silence?
Yes.
Where do you think you are now?
I'm not ... I um you have a you have children in who are under you there are your responsibility and I sometimes you know my responsibility to um make sure they get where they ought to be which is un there. Your um brother. I can't put my head I can't get it that have they got boys? And no girls. I'm not talking ...
Who are we talking about?
[Silence]
This is making you cranky?
No not at all. I'm just tired.
Do you wish me to leave and come back tomorrow?
Oh that would be lovely.
So I will come back tomorrow. Do you want some KFC in the morning?
That would be lovely.
And I'll talk to you.
Yes and you can give me a smack now and again.
[Laughter]
Ah, right-e-oh. We won't put that in the book. They would accuse me of elder abuse. Do you want me to put your feet up?
Yes please. Who show you this?
How to put the chair up? I've been doing this for over a year. Is that comfortable?
Yes. There is a little I don't know what the le but it means my spis spis spis and I am working ... [unintelligible]
You have a good sleep and I will see you tomorrow.

134

20th September 2015

If you are anything like me you are a grotty eater of KFC.
Oh lovely.
It's not too hot?
No it is good. Thank you.
You are welcome.

It is all mucked up here.
What is mucked up?
Oh we get funny things in here I somebody I forget who it was me it was me
I um um I forget I had terribly um very some things about something I got
into I did that the stuff that I had there was there and she got into some poo
I don't know I don't know why it couldn't possibility be poo so it is not poo
pieces I've got had... This is beautiful.
I'm pleased you like it.

Have you been here before?
Do you know who I am?
No. You have been before hey?
Who gave you all the photos on the wall do you know?
Not me.
No but somebody took them and gave them to you.
I don't know.

Jennifer Clarke from Kempsey did that.
Oh!
Do you remember Jennifer Clarke?
[Unintelligible]
You are going mad girl!
I said I'm not mad however today I am good.
So who am I?
You are Jenny.
I am.

I they are lovely.
The chicken?
Yeah. Are you getting your what?
I don't understand. Am I getting my what what?
Are you getting something that I don't know?
Yes I am pinching some of your chips and lollies.
I am so pleased that I are able to put up with me and different I don't know what I am trying to say ...
Your eyesight is getting worse you know?
Mmmm.
That is your drink.

Finding it hard to help me things?
Am I finding it hard?
Mmmm?
Um! I am finding it hard to watch you deteriorate.
Oh right. Well made up just you don't you worry about it.
Why?
Well when I don't any worry that that you do have you take on things mate and I'm most grateful but you you um [Sigh!] I think you wonder not good ...
I take on too much?
Yeah.
But I said that I was coming up here every month or so until you died.
No, no, no, no, yeah ...
But I do worry Mary because I love you.
If I had the money and the diddly and the whatever what's in the outside world we could go somewhere but we can't.
No.
[Unintelligible] ... but together she is the one who looks at things to see people but Jenny you [said very softly] you mean more to me ...

Yes?
You mean more to me.
You mean a lot to me, my girl. We are doing this book together.
[Laughter]
I'm sorry that you have to come over me to get my piece.
You have to come over me to get my piece?
No.
Well I'm sorry I don't know what you are saying.
She doesn't as much love in me.
I have a lot of love for you.
Yeah, yeah, yeah.
You trying to bite my finger!
[Chuckle] I something gone right.
Yeah your brain.
You think so?
[Laughter]
Yeah I think so.
Oh! That's good.
Why is it good?
I don't have to die and worry about it.
Why? Are you worrying what was going on with you?
Yeah.
You know you've got dementia!
Mmmm.
And you know that we are writing a book together. Do you remember that?
Yes.
This is a tape recorder and it tapes our conversations. I take it home and I transcribe it. When you go to God, God who is good...
I hope he is able to take the no uh...
Well you could take the tape recorder with you and tape God...
[Laughter]
... and say God what do you think of this situation? Do you think that is funny?
I do.
[Laughter]
So when you go to God I will finish the book.
Wouldn't that be funny, wouldn't that be funny if we did a nice book and it landed on the best sellers list, [Laughter], and that's what it was.
And God got a look at it and he gave his opinion. Hey, God could write the foreword!

[Laughter]

I'm sure I'm about to be hit by lightning! I'm glad you are amused by this. Hey nobody in the history of the world would have the foreword of their book written by God.

[Laughter]

I think I've gone mad!

Do you?

[Laughter]

Yep.

[Laughter]

Well I was mad yesterday so there you go.

We can be mad together. Now what would you say, a foreword by God. I'll have to sit down and think about this 'cause the only way we could get a foreword out of God would be sitting and meditating and praying and letting it come into our minds.

I think he could to go and to sit and what you were saying too for Jesus two different people, people don't think of God of being with Jesus…

Disturbed by the nurse… Knock, knock. How are you all?

Fine thank you.

As silly as she has always been.

Ha! Thank god she has left.

Did she go?

Yes she was just putting some pads in the back of the door

[Laughter]

Silly as she has always been!!!

[Laughter]

Thank you very much Sr Mary Magdalene Quinn.

Oh dear [Mary wipes her eyes]. You are getting that strong at it you don't know you are being naughty. I'm very sorry I'm doing this.

No ya not. It is good to have a laugh. We don't laugh enough in this life.

Do you think?

Well Mary you know that I am a stirrer and that I have been a stirrer all my life and I always like to make people laugh. I think that is one of the things that is missing from the bible.

You think?

Yeah. The blokes that wrote the bible were unwise not to get the female input… no let me say that better, they didn't use the input they were given from the women. One of the things that I think is missing is that there is a lot of violence and blood but there is not much humour. Let's have a few jokes in life. Life is too serious in the bible.

You got it?

What?

Working out what you are going to see.

What am I gonna see?

About some of those women ...

Oh! About putting something humorous in the bible. I think that men sometimes put women down because women are sometimes better than them at certain things.

I find it absolutely fascinating that you are holding the box with one hand, your left hand, and your right hand is still looking for the chips.

Oh!

You've gone about a foot away from where the left hand is holding the box to get to the chips. Amazing!

What's that?

It's the tape recorder.

Okay.

What would you like to see go in the book?

Oh. Is there anything in the book?

[Laugh]. I've got about 100 transcribed pages so far of our conversations and about what you think and about God and you've talked sometimes about your anger and dementia. Sometimes you think it is not fair but at other times ... um the theme that is running through the whole book is your belief that God is good.

My boy?

That your belief that God is good. So if you got the opportunity to say exactly what you wanted to say about having dementia, because this book is about you going into dementia and losing your memory, if you had the opportunity to say something ...

Mmmm!

... to go in the book what would it be? What would be the most important thing that you would like to tell the readers?

Mmmm ... Oh!

Maybe I should have asked this question 12 months ago!

Why?

Because you do not seem to have an answer for me.

You haven't got an answer?

No.

Well … is there any other cancer where is it working where is it what can you get in it?

You can get anything in it that you want. You might want to say 'I'm suffering from dementia but it does not take away from the wonderful life I've had'.

Ahm!

Or you might say 'I am looking forward to going to heaven' …

Mmmm!

'I know God is good'!

Yeah!

'And my dementia has nothing to do with my faith in Jesus'.

Yeah!

If you had the opportunity to say one thing, what would it be?

To be anything of anything?

Yes.

You want you could find somethings that you wanted to do.

So life is about something that you can do?

Yes.

Is that what you are saying?

Mmmm.

And yours was throwing chalk in maths class!

[Laughter]

Oh I'm a naughty girl.

What did you where did you come in that …

Class? I probably came last.

What about?

Maths. I was useless at maths.

By them … I think I've got an answer and asked before that um that scsssssss I asked God and good asked the answer to a question from your sister where I was going and what else she doesn't fit this very strong but um but she she didn't want to be many people this probably I'm getting because she is the one I'm talking to, not doing she being understood and that was I was about was about what is thing about and I got I think I have a a settled to women and women are women plus God is God and women are women. It is very there is a very clear thing or it was back then that women 'womened' and you wouldn't be a women um if did you did some things and you shouldn't be a women and now there's we've got quite easily women um women are women. That right.

Just fascinating …

Can you get that box and get I want to get it to come from is it on the wall?
What box are we talking about Mary?
Box box put things in ...
The chicken?
Yeah.
It's finished. It's eaten, it is gone.
Right so that's finished. Hello.
Hello.
[Laughter]
What do you feel about that?
What do I feel about what?
What you did happen threw at me.
What did I throw at you?
You was to um you were looking ... [unintelligible] ... a woman whose going out from place going from your work um ... I don't know ... anyway ... very very beautiful meal. Thank you.
You are most welcome.

[Sigh!] Oh Dear. Most interesting.
What is most interesting?
The road there. There is a lot more people talking down the road about my my you about you somebody else's do the same it is quite interesting ...
We all travel amazingly different roads.
Yeah. Don't go away please.
No. I was just getting my walking stick.

So, if you could put anything into a book that we are writing about your dementia, what would it be?
[Silence]
What are you thinking?
I'm trying to get my mesemout, something like that.
Mesemount! What does that mean?
[Silence]
Well I put um I want ... I want some people who are mercy.
People who are mercy?
Mmmm. When are you leaving?
About midday.
Ahm!
[Silence]

Mary if you were able to say anything about dementia for the book what would you say?
It's um a very reand very re re very cruel well um um re.
It is very cruel?
Yeah.
The dementia is cruel?
Yes.
Why is the dementia cruel?
Because um ah it it the um the teacher, the person, the person is hit by by um ah hit knows that somethings gone wrong and ah I don't know woo what's been in my life its its um the ah there's been no no understanding of um a bit comes around eh that what what ah is is the ah the um dementia can get.
Yeah. It is horrible.
Mmmm!

Mary, you don't look me in the eye very much now. Why is that?
Ah! [Questioning sound]
You are not looking at me now. You are looking at my arm.
No. No.
Normally you would look me in the eye but this time you have hardly done it.
Hmmm! I'm um um um…
No reason for that?
Yes. I don't think there um nameie I'm missing this…
Somebody out there is talking and it is distracting?
Yes!
Do you like listening to other people talk?
No.
Noisy is it?
Yep.
Why is it that noise makes you so irritated Mary?
Maybe ah I don't get here and comes back. I don't know…

What are you thinking Mary?
I'm trying to get eh go to the gie for the teacher who got you ah lid like to get something much there are things to be thought about and then turned into those are thought. You know what I mean?
You need a teacher to help you with something.
Yeah.

Mary just had a snooze and woke up a little agitated. She started clapping her hands.

Hoy, hoy hoy.
Why?
What do you want to do?
I want to make your ready to ah...
I think you are a bit confused. I think you just had a snooze and you just woke up.
And you think you would I go and go on.
No you are going to lunch in a minute. And then I am going to leave you.
[Garbled]
[Clapped hands again]
Here comes someone.
Where do you want to go?
I don't know. It won't be long. I'm okay.
[Clapping]
Just over there is a woman coming towards me. Keep your hands out.
So where do you want to go? What do you want a nurse for?
[Made cranky sound]
Mary, think, think. Get your brain going. You're getting agitated.
Want ta go on the top table.
You wish to get on the bed?
Yeah.
Not at the moment.
Why?
Lunch is on shortly.
Oh I didn't know that, that you could go to lunch. Hell yeah, yeah.
I'll take you out to lunch in a moment.

Can you remember what it was like before you had dementia, Mary?
No.
You don't remember what it was like?
Why, what was like?
You were able to look after yourself.
Just say it and go...
You were able to teach people, you could walk around.
Yeah.
What is it like not being able to do that?
Silly is it.
Silly is it?

Mmmm.
Frustrating?
Can't get, have you got enough ... [Garbled]

Mary started to become agitated again so I started singing Amazing Grace. Mary calmed down and joined in the singing. As an aside, we both sounded drunk!

How was that?
Not bad.
I thought you'd want to shoot me, I sounded that awful.
[Laughter]

Mary I love you.
Yeah that's right. I am not not noticing. I don't I'm not I don't have any real emotion.
What is your name?
Mary Quinn.
What is your middle name?
Mary Magdalene Quinn.
Who am I?
Mary, Mary ... I'm sorry. You're going back to Kempsey aren't you?
Yes and you won't have to answer any more questions. Do the questions hassle you?
No, not at all.
Just gets frustrating that you cannot find the answers sometimes?
No. I know what I got to that coming in well and truly in time it happens that gives somebody have to go it was sort of um ...
What would you say if this was the last time that you ever saw me?
Oh that would be sad. I wouldn't be able to I get out the gosh ...
I'll see you in three weeks.
Okay.

10th October 2015

[Garbled] ... It's cliberly a lot.
What's a lot?
Cliberly.
Cliberly?
Yeah.
What does cliberly mean?
[Laughter] I don't know.

I wrote the introduction to the book the other day.
Mmmm.
The first draft. Do you want to hear it?
Yes. I'd love it.
Well then, let me get it. It is only a draft ... I'll just put my reading glasses on. 'Conversations with Mary is not a religious book per se ... this book will be seasoned with the faith of Mary Magdalene Quinn'.
Thank you very much.
Do I sound like a writer?
Yes ... It is.

You know how when I was here last time and we were laughing about getting God to do the Foreword of the book. You know getting him to write ...

[Laughter]

... some good words about it. Do you remember that?

Yes.

Anyway I said that probably the only way that we could get God to do the Foreword of the book is if we prayed about it and meditated about it. When I went home last time, I sat on the back verandah and meditated on you and the book. What came to me was your present journey is a bit like the journey that Job took. It made me think of your struggle. Every time I have come you have talked about how 'God is good' and this journey of dementia reminded me so much of Job's journey. That is how it came to me. I am amazed that with the dementia and your memory – you have lost so much – and yet you still remember God.

[Silence]

Are you with me?

Yes. Thank you.

So, how have things been going for you?

Um. I've been thinking I thought that we had I thought that I knew Dad where do I put it. I've forgotten Ilene had been one of the girls that left not left but but the the being ah ah gone to heaven. She was I I'd forgotten I got she I thought she had gone to heaven but she had... [Garbled]

Who is Ilene, Mary?

Ilene, my sister.

Your older sister?

No. My older sister... um I don't know but I won't try to say not say about her. It was just se ah the sort the stop of the fact she dad [Garbled] ... I didn't think there was anybody else left and there was. And she thought I did and I didn't one day I was I could have cried all day.

You could have cried all day?

Yeeees.

It is hard isn't it?

Mmmm.

So you forgot that she died?

Yes.

And then you remembered and that made you sad again?

Yeah. And I thought I I had thought she was alive. She wasn't.

Yeah! So when you go to God and go to heaven you will have her waiting there for you.

Yes.

That is exciting.

Yes.
What would you talk about?

Interrupted by the nurse.

Mary? Mary where are you?
Where am I! I was thinking where I was.
What you would say to Ilene when you got to heaven.
Muuum no. No I was thinking maybe your sending your giving or doing [Garbled] ... or whatever you were doing. [Silence] I like what you wrote.
You like what I wrote?
Mmmm!
Thank you Mary.
Yeah.
God is good!
God is good! Even through the pain and struggle ...
Mmmm! ... God is good. I'm gonna kick him when I see him though.
[Laughter]
That is very, very good.
Yeah. I think he deserves a good kick.
[Laughter]
He doesn't! It is not he who does it.
No. So who does it?
[Sigh] I don't know.
It is just life isn't it?
Mmmm. [Silence]

So, what would you say when you got to heaven Mary?
I would hand hand my ... I would put my hand ...
Together and hit him?
No!
Genuflect?
No. Never thought of that. I would just go up to him ...
You would honour him?
Yes.
What would you say?
Thank you for all you have done for me. Thank you God.
[Silence]

I need to go to bed.
You want to sleep for a while?

Yes.

Okay. I'll turn off the recorder and read my book. I'll wake you up in half an hour. Is that okay?

Yes.

It is now 11.30. Mary has been asleep since 10.30. I have tried to wake her a few times but she won't wake. She is obviously exhausted and yet she has been sleeping really well. I started singing and she woke up.

How are you feeling?

Okay.

Still feeling tired?

Nope.

[Silence]

When you go to heaven what do you think you will say to Ilene when you see her?

Um! Hello.

Hello! That's reasonable.

[Laughter]

I'm glad to see you.

Are you excited about seeing them?

Ah yes all of them.

All of them?

Mmmm.

It will be interesting to see what heaven is like?

Mmmm.

My thought of heaven is going up to heaven and walking along a nice country road in early summer or late spring and coming up to an old country pub and seeing Dad and my family sitting on the verandah and drinking and talking to a lot of other like-minded people.

That would be your dad wouldn't it?

That would be his heaven. Everybody has different ideas of heaven. What is your idea of heaven, Mary?

[Silence]

Did you go back to sleep on me?

I don't know.

What do you think heaven would be like, besides all the people that you love?

[Silence]

Just a like, thinking about um I tried to get tha police behind heaven.
Do you think there would be police in heaven?
No.
I think there would be a lot of happiness.
Oh yes.
I think we would understand each other a lot better.
[Silence]

[Garbled] ... did he get there yesterday?
I don't know Mary. I got here today from Kempsey. Do you know my name?
Yes. Um! I don't think I do know your name.
Are we friends?
Yes.
Do we love each other?
Yes.
But you can't remember my name.
I can't.
That is okay. It is Jennifer.
Jennifer.
Yeah. Jennifer Clarke.
I didn't know Jennifer would be a pretty name.
I'm a pretty girl.
[Laughter]
What?!
[Laughter]
Don't sound so surprised Mary Quinn.
Are you?
Am I pretty? I've never thought much about that. I don't think I'm ugly.

You're not a girl!
What am I, if I am not a girl?
I don't know. Are you a girl?
Charming!
[Laughter].
She's known me for 45 years and she is asking me if I'm a girl. Yes, I'm a girl. Born a girl. Raised a girl ... Um! Well, Mum tried anyway.
Are are you a girl to be honest?
What did ya think I was, a boy?
Yeah!

Jennifer Clarke is a boy. I think I'm ... I'm truly shocked, sister!
Yes, so am I.
[Laughter]
Well, this has been a most startling conversation.
Well that is fantastic!
It's fantastic that I am a girl?
Yes.
Don't you remember me being in the convent with you?
Yees.
You don't think that they would let blokes go into the convent would they?
No.
Well there you go. Then that must mean that I am a girl. True?
True.
Well there you go.

How many children do you have?
You don't remember this but I do not have children. I never got married.
You don't have children?
Nope, and thank the Lord that I don't have children.
But your dad ...
There are three sisters and one brother...
Are you a girl?
Yes. I am a girl. Would you like a look?
No.
[Laughter]
Why are you shocked that I am a girl?
I'm shocked that I didn't know.
Don't I sound like a girl?
Ah. That is probably the reason why.
I don't sound like a girl?
Ah. What the thing is that um you are a girl!
I find this ... let's get over this Mary, I'm a girl and I am not going to wear a dress to convince you either.
Isn't that interesting!
It is!
Did you like being a girl?
Yes I like being a girl. I don't think I would like to be a bloke. I've been able to have more to do with you, being a girl. You got to teach me as a child. That is how I first met you. Otherwise we would not have met.
Oh! I'm sorry.

Nothing to be sorry about. It is all quite astonishing.
[Silence]

Okay. I am going to go. I'll see you tomorrow with KFC. I love you Mary.
I love you.
You look confused.
I am.
Why?
I think it might have been when you are um the stuff around your father treated [garbled] ...

11th October 2015

Morning Mary. Here is the KFC.
I can smell it.
You can smell the KFC?
Beautiful. What about the girls?
I only got it for you.
Oh.
[Silence while eating]
Who's he?
Who, me? I am Jennifer.
That's is I can't see?
Can you hear my voice?
Yes.
Well you are looking straight at me. I am Jennifer and I am not a he.
Mmmm.
I may be wearing a flannelette shirt...
Yeah you have.
... but I always wear a flannelette shirt.
Where ya go...
Where am I going? Not going anywhere. I am sitting here and helping you to eat your chicken.
Where is it?
[Silence while eating]

How are you?
I am good.
That's good.
How is my beautiful lady?
Um, very strange.
You feel very strange?
Yeah. I've been leap…thinking this morning about Dad dying…[Mary started to cry]
You forgot that your dad had died?
No.
Just the pain hit you again?
Mum had gone…
So mum had gone, dad had gone and Ilene had gone.
No Ilene had not gone.
She was still alive when your dad had gone?
Yes.
[Silence]

I don't know who…it to have people around you.
It is nice to have people around you?
[Silence]

[Garbled]…Dads die and where were you?
Where did I live when my dad died? I lived in Kempsey.
I remember.
Do you remember the funeral?
No.
You came in the church and sat way up the back. I had to go looking for you and bring you up the front with the family.
Oh!
[Silence]

Why did you ask about Dad's funeral and me living in Kempsey?
I ah was being after my dad on my dad was much farther back than your dad…
Yes your dad died before mine.
I should be giving your other friend some of this.
No I brought it for you.

Mary, am I a girl or a boy?

I think you are a girl.
Thank God for small mercies. Yesterday...
You're my friend.
Yes. Yesterday when I was here you insisted that I was a boy.
I didn't!
[Laugh]. Yes you did.
Did I?
You did. It was most amusing.
Oh that is awful.
No it's not awful. I was just wondering where it was coming from and if you would remember it today. And we had another conversation about going to heaven. I asked what you would say to Ilene and you said you would say hello.
[Laughter]
And I thought, oh well that is fair enough. I said that if I ever seen God I'd kick him in the knee caps.
[Laughter]
I'm such a nasty brute.
What made you think I thought...
What made you think I was a boy? I have no idea.
Mmmm.
[Garbled]... I knew always that you were a girl.
Yeah. I think yesterday you were having a really tough time. You were really tired and you spent most of the time sleeping while I was here. And then when you woke up that was when you insisted I was a boy. You must have been dreaming something strange!
[Laughter, then silence]

When you were into what you were eating is the I was eating I never be um eating prayers on our... there was always... [Garbled]... I've never had egg on it.

So, if you said hello to God when you went to heaven, what do you think God would say to you?
[Garbled]
You know what I think he would say?
What?
Well done, good and faithful servant!
Thank you.
Do you think that is what he would say?

[Shrug]
I think God would.

I remember, I think you was the first time I talked to you and it was about you father who was a bit of a ah drinker ... is that right?
Dad was a bit of a drinker Mary. I'm amazed that you can remember that.
And your mother at the time was very bad in um she was trying to um she was very very um bad in bed because she was heading for heaven. And I see her in the room that she was in. That's interesting; any time that I am talking to you I remember where your mother was.
When she was dying?
Mmmm.

Where are we?
St Michael's in Casino. You would rather be in Grafton the nurses said to me this morning.
Yes. I don't know where that place is.
Where mum died?
No. Where we talk about now.
St Michael's?
I don't know. I don't know St Michael's.
Well you have been here for a number of years.
Okay. I'm not putting you out?
No. Why would you be putting me out?
[Garbled]

I can't imagine what ...
St Michael's?
Yeah.
Why can't you imagine St Michael's?
Well I never really can tell anything when you can get Tullymorgan or the um Grafton where I were in the ... I want to go to bed!
Well how about you close your eyes and have a snooze and I will wake you up in half an hour. How does that sound?
That you are a beautiful lady.
Yeah, I take after you!

Ah there is something something out of this ah when we were little kids we were grandfather ah when we go to anywhere we ar Dad had done Dad had died and ah we go to people where there were only kids so I wasn't wasn't ah

155

I don't all my life I've ah not owing um boys I didn't boys...until I came until my later life where I in school I met boys...

Mary had a short visit from a friend.

Well there you are!
That was quick.
Have you got, got short short...
Hair? Yes.
It is lovely.
You'd be the only one your age that would reckon that. My Aunty Marie would like to get me and shake me when I cut my hair off.
How is that Aunty? Still alive?
She is 86 and still going well. Still does a bit of milking. She is an amazing lady.
Yeah. Are you going to go first or...
First where?
Here. [Garbled]...

Do you remember who the lady was that just came and visited you?
Nope.
[Silence]

There is a lady same name lady who's been in ages for going to um she she the ah I don't know what I'd call it. She was a lonely person and then she was ah she came in the other day and I spoke to her and the name is the same and the name or something like that.
Jenny?
No. Not you Jenny.
I don't know who you are talking about Mary, sorry.
Why?
Why am I sorry?
Yeah.
I don't know. I'm just being polite. I'm not polite most of the time so I'd take it if I were you.
[Laughter]
What is making you smile? You look like the Cheshire Cat.
[Mary made a strange noise and then started laughing].
Can't get it! They were connected to each other and they were who where they the um [sigh] where the [Garbled]...the way through ahem no one would be able to [Garbled]...the at lady at the end and then you could put in

156

the next lists and it would be long ... laugh ... look at that face ...

A very noisy person walks past.

Hello!
Hello!
Who's there?
Uh! I don't know.
Don't worry, nor do I.
[Laughter]
Oh you are on a roll Mary.
[Laughter]

You get a name now and again?
Mmmm.
And it flashes through your mind?
No. On my finger.
What was that?
On my finger.
You've got a name on your finger?
Yeah.
Fascinating!
[Laughter]
What is so funny?
I don't know. I just say it.
[Silence]

30th October 2015

What are you talking about?
Funny fellow ...
[Laughter]
Do you remember E.H.?
Nope.
R.C.
Ummmmm ... no.
P.B.
She is in heaven.
A.H.
Who?
A.H.
Who is that?
Do you remember Jenny Clarke?
Yep.
Who is she?
You.
[Silence]

What are you thinking?
Nothing.
Are you enjoying the music?

I'm enjoying what she is doing.

Oh dear my leg is going to fall off.
Oh was I leaning on it. Is that better?
Might be.
[Groan]
Which leg?
That leg. Can't get up.
[Groan]
That hurt?
Yes!
Sorry.
[I massage the leg]
Is that better?
Yes.
Was it cramping?
Don't know.
Is that enough or should I continue doing it?
[Mary nods vigorously]
Thanks. My hand is going to fall off now. Your leg won't, but my hand will.
[Laughter]
She'll be right...

I hope you come before you go home.
Um! What? You hope I come before I go home?
Yes.
Okay. I will try and figure out what that means in a minute.

Nope! What does that mean?
There's a skid four or five schools around here—Catholic.
Are there?
Mmm. And ones actually I think it is where I live now or just for a lightener, I don't lie it is um um did the kids for um um...and [Garbled]...A big kids go out.
Mary, is God good?
[Silence]

Did your brother come with you?
Does who come with me?
I don't know.

159

Mary, who is God?
No one.
God is no one? Do you know what that means?
No!
You don't know who God is?
I do know who God is.
Mm-hmm!
He is that person in the world that looks after you to go to the world … He maded Mary and is a wonderful man …

What is your name?
Um! To be honest I don't know.
Mm-hmm. Does Mary Clarke sound right?
Yes.
Oh! What about Mary Jones?
Don't know.
What about Mary Quinn?
That is my name.
What about Mary Magdalene Quinn?
Yes!

You would like to sit here and do what?
I would like to sit here with you.
Well I will sit here and stay with you.

So how is R. Have you seen her lately?
She is here in this place.
R.?
Yeah.
So she has come back from her trip?
Yeah.

I have begun to notice that if I ask you about a person's name outright you don't know them, but if I say something about the person, without asking you a question about who they are, you seem to know them. I find that really interesting.
Mm-hmm
I will put that in the book that we are writing together.
Okay.

Music is playing in the background.

This is a sing-song story and my sister Ilene used to sing this.
Your sister Ilene who has gone to God?
I hope so.
Why? Do you think she has been naughty?
[Laughter]
I don't think she has.
I don't think she has either. She is your sister. I don't think she would have been naughty.
[Silence]

What are you thinking?
I've been thinking of habits how the young people who don't go get on.
How the young people don't get on with each other?
Yeah.
Many young people are like that through any generation, I reckon.
What's that?
I said that most people would be like that through any generation.
[Silence]

[Garbled]…I have some soooo ah is the aim when she is in St Joseph is my place. Was Saint the school…
St Joseph's is in Kempsey.
No was it in is it Australian is in…
Oh! There is a Sisters of St Josephs!
No…but…
So what about St Joseph's?
Here?
No. There is no St Joseph's here.
Oh!
All I know of connected with St Joseph's is the Blacks, the Browns and St Joseph's in Kempsey but that is not what you are talking about is it?
No.
Are you talking about Mary's husband?
No no no that's the answer I know has got it doesn't know.
It doesn't know!
No.
Right.
Joseph is there because the lady who set up Joies…
It must have been an amazing experience setting up an order of religious sisters.

Yes.

Back in 18th century onwards. What would it have been like for Catherine!!! Or for all those Sisters who came out from Ireland? To go from the cold climate of Ireland to the heat of summer in Grafton. What a shock it must have been! The culture shock must have been amazing also.

Yes!

They were very brave women.

Yes!

[Break]

What did you say?

I said that I have just as bad a memory as you and yet you get fed with a comfortable chair in a nice building, while I get nothing. That went straight over your head and parted your hair on the way through.

I don't know.

Don't worry about it Mary. I am just being a naughty girl ... as I've always been.

Hah!

Naughty till the day I die!

Yeah well I was gonna say jump over into bad.

Jump over into bad! Thanks Mary. I love you too.

[Laughter]

I wonder something that what would be with you and I are together when we have ah ...

When you go to God?

Yeah!

Would you like to be together?

I'd love it!

We could tell bad jokes.

No you can't!

We could drive God insane.

[Laughter]

Could you imagine driving God insane?

[Laughter]

No.

I could work on it every day. I could plan on telling the worst jokes in the universe. Do you think God would run from us?

[Laughter]

Or do you think God would hit me with a bolt of lightning and send me to purgatory.

162

No. no, no. He would never do that.
Oh!
God would never hit you.
Wouldn't he?
Nope.
Oh! What do you think he would do if he hated my bad jokes?
He would joke with the jokes.
He would laugh about it too you would reckon?
Yes.
Fair enough but I still like the idea of driving God insane. It has got a certain ring about it.
What?
Nothing. I'm just being naughty.

Are you going to leave the laves for the ladies?
Am I going to leave the laves for the ladies?
Mm-hmm.
I'm not really sure I understand what that means?
I think that'd be two more or less taken on a a a a a- Is that you?
Yeah.
Yeah now when you decide to take yes I'll go, I'll go quick. That's not true the the you have to turn around and go on the side.
Are you talking about when you go to God?
Hey?
Are you talking about when you go to God?
No. I am talking about how what goes for eat and [garbled] ... what the ladies are about here.
Oh.
Laaily.
Hey?
Laaily.
[Laughter]
You know it's nice.
What's nice?
Lal Lal.
Lal Lal. Who is Lal Lal?
Yeah. Lal lal lal lal lal lal lal laaa.
La La!

So, when you go to God, what are you gonna say to him?

163

I'm not doing that I'm having him come to me.
He's going to you?
He's going to come to see me.
Oh! He is coming to see you!
Yes.
So, what are you going to say to Him when He comes to see you?
Oh Lord. Jump up and say, 'Hi Jesus. I've been waiting for you'.
[Laughter]
'Jesus I've been waiting for you'. Wow! Good on ya.
[Laughter]

And what took you so long?
No I don't... he knows that he has got so many things do and then he won't be able to have that much...
Well you've still got you sense of humour Mary.
Did you think I didn't have any?
No. I know that you've got a sense of humour.
Yeah.
[Break]

'Have this got a bit of difference between it?' I don't understand what you are trying to say Mary?
Does that hap where does sigh look you've got a plat that a this ah is flat but this is got a plate... oh dear God!
What is oh dear God?
Hey?
What is oh dear God?
Oh dear God?
Yes, you said oh dear God.
Ah! I have to, there is so much around me and you and other people less in the present who are we have a lot of a lot to go through is that right?
Yes, you do go through a lot.
Yes.

Do you remember what you are in here for?
In here?
Yes. Do you know what you have got?
In here?
Yeah?
Don't know.

164

Do you remember that you've got dementia?
Yeah but I don't care what goes anymore.
You don't care anymore?
I don't care anymore! See thing that um I um I got lots of frits... [Garbled]... and I noticed that there were people who were um were a go along pick that up please and sometimes somewhere the same place somebody passes off or somebody picks up there four different things that the people that went with what I had up. So I've tried to take a lot go one or I wouldn't go there okay.
Yep.

Are you wanting to go to God soon?
No.
Are you comfortable where you are?
Yeah. Yeah.

What are you thinking?
I can't there are a lot of things. I notice that there are things that do or away things that then I know that is so and it doesn't get a... dear God my knee is killing me.
Which one?
Left one.

I begin to massage her knee.

Is that helping?
Yes. Now when are you... that's quite nice having the place put that out.
You want me to stop?
No! That's good. It's good.

When will I meet you again?
I am coming tomorrow with some Kentucky Fried.
Oh that's right. How could I go no.

What's ya going in ya other reg egg head?
What was that sorry Mary?
Nother it [laugh] no wait a minute my my doesn't bad in the next knee.
It is not as bad as in the next knee?
Yeah.

Is that enough for your knee? Can I stop now?

Yes.
Good my arm was about to fall off.
[Laughter]
Oh you liked that joke!
[Laughter]
Hey Mary?
Yeah
I love you.
I love you too.
Do you remember my name today?
Jenny.
That is the first time that you have remembered my name without a prompt for a while.
What did I say is your name?
Jenny. So if you don't think too hard about it you can usually get it or if you are in the middle of a conversation you can also say it without thinking.
Mm-hmm.
It is interesting how dementia works.
Yes.

... I get cranky about my ears.
Yeah you get cranky about a lot of things these days, don't you?
Do I? I don't know.
No. No. You've calmed...
Is that true?
... down a lot.
You're a cranky person.
I'm a cranky person? Yeah I'm cranky.
Me! Me. Me. Me.
Oh you! Ahm. When you were a teacher you were cranky at times.
Yeah.
When you were first told that you had dementia you got pretty cranky about that. You were upset.
Yeah.
Then you got cranky with the way you were brought over here to St Michaels. And every so often you got cranky as the dementia started to take you and you couldn't remember things. You go cranky with the noise. So yeah, you can get cranky.
Mm-hmm.
I'd be damn cranky about that too. You are not cranky now. I think it is

because you are too tired. Your batteries are running flat. Do you feel that?
Yeah.
But that is okay isn't it?
Yes.
You feel comfortable about going to God whenever God takes you?
Yeah.
You are taking the journey of Job.
The journey of who?
Job.
Who's Job?
Job from the bible who was tested by the devil to see if he would remain faithful to the Lord.
Oh yeah! Mm-hmm. I must read that book properly. You might read to me.

I had a beautiful experience last night.
Yes?
In my mind I met that might be what you are talking about, he someone wondered what had what happened to the lady and where is she going to get...
So it was a beautiful experience?
Yeah.
Do you think you were talking to God?
Yeah!
Do you think he was calling you home?
Yeah.
It felt calm.
[Mary nodded her head] Mm-hmm!
You felt good about it? You felt at peace?
Mm-hmm.
What a great experience to remember. And you have such a peaceful look on your face now. How about I pull your nose?
[Laughter]

Mary shapes up to me.

I'm sorry for stirring you.
You're not stirring me.
Well what am I doing?
We are having a fun together.
Mary that was a wonderful dream to have.
Mm-hmm. It wasn't wasn't a dream.

Was it a dream or a vision?
No the person didn't speak to me ah I it was a very long sing out I came out where something came in my mind and I had to think of it and think of it out. Yeah. As a matter of fact I am cap I think it was C. was a … [Garbled] … the children and um one of the she came out very hard good.

31st October 2015

Mary is visited by two other friends while I am there.

What is happening?
Are you coming?
Yeah I'm coming. I'm here. I'm just here sitting with you sharing the silence.
Yeah.
[Groan]
Are you okay?
[Silence]
Do you remember the visitors that you just had?
Oh yes. They were good.
Can you remember their names?
Yes. You, ah I think I remember their names. What are you thinking to do?
I am just going to sit here for another half hour and then I am going back to Kempsey. I will be back in four weeks, unless you decide to go to God.
Yes.
What are you going to do?
I know.
You know! What then?
I know you will stay here but I will miss you but I'll love you I'll miss you.
I'll miss you too Mary.

I am very tired.

You just go to sleep Mary.
I just ahead where in we were going out. I um what's her name H. talked to her about um ah the lady around Jesus.
Mary?
Yes?
You said the lady around Jesus–Magdalene?
Yeah.
Um!
What do you mean?
I don't know. I was trying to follow your conversation but obviously I was very wrong.
Why?
Because I didn't get it and I confused you.
No. No. I wasn't lost that way. She said that um she had to have a conversation amongst a lot of people around somebody being somebody that I knew know and the Mary not a Mary at all it was something this lady had gone up to see Mary she is very close to dying. She is before Jesus.
She is before Jesus. You mean she has gone to God?
Yeah
I?
Oh no, no, no. The Jesus before I don't know. I this lady would not be dead she told me she is not and the ladies name is … [Garbled] … My head is so full I can't remember what's ah maybe …
What is your head so full of Mary?
What happens who has before heaven her mother who goes to heaven is her story is or what I don't want to be tired …
You don't want to be tired when you go to heaven?
No that is neat.
I think that you will be up and jumping and dancing when you go to heaven.
[Laughter]
You will no longer be in this body. Your spirit will be free and light
I hope so.
You hope so?
I was so happy R. was there.
It was good to see her.
I am so glad you are here.
I am so glad that I am too.
So, I'll say good night.

I don't know that I am very very time that I see you I say Jesus I am just trying

to I know I have a ... God and something I don't know what I do ...
[Long period of silence]

Can I take my table?
What table are we discussing?
I don't know. These people are doing things they can know themselves.
They can know themselves?
Mm-hmm.
Not many people know themselves. It takes a lot of work to get to know yourself doesn't it?
Mm-hmm.
You were very good at that.
Yes she is.
Jen is gonna go then.
Okay.
I'll pray for you when I head back.

The peace of the Lord Jesus Christ be with you always.
Amen.
And if you go to God before I come back, have a good journey and make sure you go first class. And have a nice glass of champagne on the way through the Gates.
Okay.

1st November 2015

Because I was concerned for Mary's health I made a decision to pop back in on my way through to Kempsey.

I think it sad that maybe our last conversation will be an argument about chocolate milk.
Mm-hmm.
Isn't life grand!
Isn't it.
Could you imagine all the 40 years we've spent together as friends?
Yes.
And one of the very last conversations we will ever have in life is about chocolate milk. Who would figure that?
Mm-hmm.
I'd rather talk about something like the meaning of life.
Yes.
Or what God would say to you when you went to heaven.
He will live forever.
Amen. Why do you think God will live forever?
I don't know.
It is a question of faith isn't it?
Mm-hmm.

Are you uncomfortable?

No.
Good
I'm wanting to get to bed.
I don't know why they take you out of bed half the time.

28th November 2015

We're getting, we're getting are ... the energy and the people and I wrote here with energy for good people take a lot of time and ah ... it'll be lovely pick it up ...

Someone sent you a money note of Catherine McCauley (Irish currency).
Aha!

'Love from L.'. Who is L.?
No.

'Mary, Sursum Corda'.
Ah!

Do you know what Sursum Corda means?
No.

I'll have to look it up. It's probably something Latin ...

We got an interesting thing this morning.

What happened this morning?
In this place kids are making things of how they and he was a nice man ... [Garbled]

So do you remember what we are doing together?
Yes.

What are we doing together?
Today is ... [garbled] ...

[Mary snickers]

What is amusing you?

You've got so much and so wonderful ahm that you are back here. Have you got to go back?

I only just got here but yes I've got to go back but I will be back tomorrow.

There are so there is a nice ah there might be two of them boys here getting on here he is as good as you one of them.

Yeah!

What's his name? I cannot remember it.

I'm not sure who you are talking about Mary.

Your sister, where would she be?

My sister lives in Lismore.

Is she well?

Yes she is pretty good. My brother said to say g'day to you.

Thank you. I'm read about ahm yes yes yer sister …

Why are you worried about my sister?

She's at the girl ahm who she's ah got it ah a chip not a chip ahm a lot lot of problem in her I don't whether she knows she's on another place but I don't know whether she has hurt her leg or what.

I am not sure what you are talking about Mary.

Do you remember last time I was here and I asked you the question "Mary what are you gonna say to God when you go to heaven?"

Yes.

Do you remember what you said?

I don't think so.

You said to me something like this "Well in this instance God is coming to me and I am going to say, hi Jesus. I've been waiting for you"

Ah!

[Laughter]

I nearly fell off my seat laughing.

[Laughter]

It's pretty good isn't it?

It is. Yes there is no worth giving them worrying about what they do or don't do because that's …

There is no use worrying about what God is going to do?

Yeah!

I'm sure that he will want to put me somewhere where he doesn't have to hear me tell bad jokes.

175

[Laughter]
You like that one?
Yes.

So, how are you feeling?
Good.
You look very tired.
Yes, yes I've been looking out for this fellow and sorting it out.

You are not good.
Yes I am in a bit of pain. But that is life. We all have our little challenges to live with.
Up and down.
Yep. Exactly
Who, you do the whole thing don't you?
What whole thing?
Yeah you're the whole own the who I've what you've got there?
I'm not sure what you mean Mary?
Oh! Maybe I don't know you.
Maybe you don't!
Yeah.
Do you know my name?
I don't know.

The um …
If I told you I came from Kempsey …
Yeah.
Would that give you any idea who I might be?
[Silence]
I bet you if I told you that you used to throw chalk at me …
[Laughter]
Oh you poor man!
You poor man!!! Thanks Mary!
[Laughter]
Poor girl.
[Laughter]
Don't worry.
It's the dementia?
Yes it is … dementia. I can't get that word.
You sometimes like to call it demuntia.

Mm-hmm.

Whatever it is called it is a nasty illness.

It is.

Yeah. Yeah.

It just takes you and you get no, no, no, no, no, no, no, no, no, no, no!!!

It just takes you!

Yeah.

Where does it take you Mary?

Um. I do get I can speak about it. I can help people about it. I can take the people who are getting in it there is quite a number of them.

Does it still make you angry?

No. I do I do. I'm I but some people get into it and don't know what they are talking about. But a lot of them do now so its but it's bad for me 'cause I cannot I get to say to somebody and I cannot ... but ...

You've lost what you are trying to say?

Yes! Yeah!

And that is very frustrating.

Yeah.

So do you remember throwing the chalk in class?

No I don't.

[Laughter]

Dead-eye Mary.

[Laughter]

Oh dear!

What are you oh dear-ing?

I am doing stuff. I am thinking of something that's not helping me ... I'm happy doing things. I'm a bit worried about the other lady whose ... how's she related to you?

The one with the bad back?

Yes.

That's me.

Ah no no it's not the other one. Ah ...

The one who comes up from Kempsey every month to see you?

No.

That idiot! [Laugh]

[Laugh] I should punch you but I can't.

You should punch me ... why should you punch me Mary?

You're hands are on there and your other ones are on there and I bit ...

177

I could reach over and pull your nose.
[Mary pretends to cry]
Oh you are good.
[Laughter]
Oh dear!

How long are you staying?
I am only up for the weekend.
Oh that is you I am go I be good with you.
Sigh! I am very tired as are you. Our batteries are running down Mary.
Oh dear mostly not for me. Honestly.
Well you are on the bed and asleep half the time.
[Laughter]
Well I can be can be that.

So, do you know who I am yet?
Yes, yes … the strange one.
[Laughter]
The straaange one!!!
[Laughter]
Have you always thought of me as strange?
Yes … No!
Oh! Okay. You are lucky that you said that. That's really funny Mary.
Well it was before it's when you were speaking you were saying um not not sticking ah it there a couple of pillow on the other side I getting itchy. I think had a bad morning.

There is something I am trying to get into out of …
Can you pull it out of your brain?
No I think this is can you hear this fellow?
I can hear a bloke outside yeah. Do you like that bloke?
No. I don't know him. She there is a fellow she loves but she in not her … she is not on her way but that is her … him …

So, did you cope with the heat?
I did. I couldn't believe it. The day that it was the best day I got up and some [Garbled] … and I didn't even see it.

Who did you have ah …
Who am I?

No. Do you know who you are?
[Laughter]

That is a lovely song.
It is.
I think it's Irish.
That's probably why you like it.

What is there not to like about Mary Magdalene Quinn?
[Mary smiles]
You have a lovely smile Mary.
Have I?
You do.
Ah dear!

I wonder where someone got that singing?
There is a record playing out there somewhere.
Yeah. Yeah. And it is not Australian.
I think it is Irish.

Are you sick?
No. I'm just tired. It took a lot of energy to drive up here.
You'll be here tomorrow won't you?
Yes, and I'll bring the KFC.
Okay. You are a very lovely, loving person.
Thank you. Thank you very much. And I think you are an amazing lady. You have done so much for the Lord here on Earth. You have helped a lot of people.
Of children who have walked into people. You know the ones.
The kids from St Josephs?
No. There was a lady, a girl who called up I called her up and put her in a place and it she went to on one of my nieces and I got her in and it's there still helping them. There is one of them I love.
One of your nieces?
No. no. These people these girls ...
That you helped?
Yes. Down the line anyway. She is lovely going anyway ...

I always go up when I hear my de ma parents ... [Garbled] ... but I loved them that's ...

Can you sometimes hear your parents talk to you?
I beg your pardon?
Can you sometimes hear your parents talk to you?
No.

Can you hear God calling you home?
Mm-hmm.
You can?
Mm-hmm.
So, you are not going to go yet?
Nope!
When are you going to go?
When you are ready to go.
When I am ready to go?
Mm-hmm.
You are going to wait for me to go with you?
No. No. You go.
You want me to go to heaven?
I go you go.
But I do not want to go to heaven just yet. I'm not ready to die just yet.
No.
I'm 25 years younger than you. Can I hang around a little while longer?
Yes. I give you permission.
[Laughter]
I am so pleased. So you wish to wait until I am ready to go? That might be another 10 years Mary.
Mm-hmm.
Do you think you can stand hanging around in this chair for another 10 years?
Could!
You could? Wow!
I keep her been helping you.

I'll give you a day.
When you are gonna go?
[Laughter]
Yes choose.
You are going to choose a day?
No.
What does that mean then?

That is what you did.
Who did? Me?
Yeah.
That I am making you choose a day?
[Laughter]
Oh! I apologise.
No. No.
I'm not trying to get rid of you or anything.
I know that.
I'm just wondering if you feel ready to go?
No, no, no, no, no.
Mm-hmm.

I'd be very lonely.
You've been very lonely?
I would be.
Going to heaven?
Mm-hmm.
Why? You've got your mum and dad there. You…
Haven't!!! In heaven you mean?
Yeah.
Oh!
Where do you think they would be if they weren't in heaven?
Oh they'd be in heaven.
Yeah.
But I'd I'd no come to you in heaven.
I'd come looking for you in heaven too—but there would be so many people up there who would be looking forward to seeing you that I wouldn't get a word in edgewise for at least 25 years.
[Laughter]
Oh dear.
You'd be yak, yak, yak, yak catching up on all of the gossip.
Mm-hmm.
Enjoying the afterlife and P.B., she'd—well neither of you—would take a pause for breath.
Actually somebody brought me in something about to I don't know how she came to think it…
Don't know. And then there is a lot of sisters who you would remember and your sister Irene who'd also be waiting to say g'day. My mum would also want a word. You remember my mum?

I do very well. I liked her a lot.

I actually liked her a lot too. Although she was a bit of a pain in the neck when I was a kid.

[Laughter]

But when I grew up I appreciated her more.

I like your dad. Poor old fellow.

Snort! Dad was 80 this year so you are three or four years older than dad.

Um! Your dad is in heaven isn't he?

Well I'd like to think so.

Listen who … wait a minute … Another person out there doing what we are doing?

Talking?

Yeah. Talking about their relatives that are gone …

… she is a nice lady and she just not Ireland she is Australian and she is an … girl take to Ireland.

I know you went and worked in Ireland for a while.

It was beautiful.

Yes, you told me that you loved it.

What are you thinking Mary?

There is a thing in the direction of the R. she he might have been looking at her.

Who is R.?

E. There is something over the other side of the light. Ireland is very close to Australia.

We are because of our Catholicity.

No.

Well, I think our church owes its existence to the priests and nuns who came out from Ireland. That is what I am saying.

Yes.

The first nuns that populated the Sisters of Mercy here in Grafton were from Ireland.

Mm-hmm. And I lost my dad!

Why are you thinking of your dad now?

He is dead.

Yes I know and he has been gone for a long time now.

Don't push that please.

No I was moving it to try and get comfortable.

I started telling Mary about what was being written in the Bilum magazine.

Oh. That is alright. Good things.
They do good things don't they?
Mm-hmm.
You know you only have to touch one person and it is worth all of the money that the organisation puts into these people. It is amazing what one person can do.
Yeah.
How one person can change another's life.
Yeah. Now what do you do?
What do I do now?
Yeah.
I'm gonna go home and go to bed. Is that okay with you?
Yes!
I'll come back tomorrow?
If you are right and it is more for you.
I want to come back and ask you heaps more questions.
Okay.
Like mirror, mirror on the wall is Mary Quinn the smartest one of all?
[Laughter]
Ah there…
[Laughter]

That was pretty good wasn't it?
[Laughter]
It was.

What will you do?
Think about the questions I want to ask you. What would be the question if it was the last that I could ever, ever ask you? I would probably ask: has living life in the service of God been worth the journey?
Mm-hmm.
Do you understand the question?
I don't know.
Okay let me ask it in a different way if I can. You've lived your life as a Sister of Mercy in the service of God and Jesus looking after people on earth that you have come in contact with. Has your life been worth it?
Oh yes!!!
And why do you say yes so emphatically?

183

Well um it's the thing that the person that is asking for they want it they need it they want to give other people the opportunity.

They want to give other people the opportunity?

No not they want...

I think what you are trying to say is that you want to help people find their way in life like you were given the opportunity to find your way in life. Is that what you are trying to say?

Mm-hmm.

You want to help them find their potential in life?

Well I haven't had an opportunity at this time ahm its its um haven get the you have to be yourself as well as the other pieces because you are moving on too.

Yeah my battery is flattening too.

Mm-hmm.

I'm tired and I'm sure that you know what that feels like.

No!

You don't get exhausted?

No.

[Laughter]

I must be in a bad way then.

[Laughter]

You've got the um ah other thing under us?

The pain?

Yes.

The pain is tiring.

I have no pain.

You have no physical pain?

Yes.

[Mary is actually on pain patches.]

Do you have emotional pain?

No. No. I uh I think I've got the aptitude to I and a does what it the other person who picks it up and I have that opportunity. Like you were those needs being answered there this morning that what um that's doing um is me the opportunity.

The opportunity to serve God?

Mm-hmm.

I love you Mary.

I love you.

May the Lord bless you. May the Lord keep you and may the Lord shine his

face upon you and say well done good and faithful servant.
Thank you.
Amen.
Amen.

29th November 2015

… you went to communion.
What did you find?
That you got Jesus stuck to the roof of your mouth.
[Laughter]
Oh dear it was terrible.
Was it?
Yes
I get Jesus stuck to the roof of my mouth occasionally too.

Do you want to take me to the doctor?
No, I don't want to take you to the doctor.
What do you want to do?
Sit here and look at ya!
[Laughter]
It is Sunday and the doctor is not open.

Um things in these things that we wouldn't have they come the line they would have taken meals to somebody.
I've been bringing KFC to you every Sunday that I come. Little did I know many years ago that you liked junk food.
What!
That is junk food.

Is it?

Yes. You probably would never have got much of it back when you were in the convent.

Do you know Eric E.?

You seem to have a focus on this Eric E. bloke.

That's right.

Why are you focused on him? You have never met him before in your life.

No.

So what is it about him?

I don't know the man. Um he I came to him because he came to me and I was um Mary and the young people seem to hang onto Ilene. That is why it happened. [Mary started to cry] Ilene died. She was a little girl and she died.

How old was Ilene when she died?

About 8. Oh dear.

God did take her home early.

Dad, Mum, Ilene...

Do you think you will be next?

No I don't think so... In the last few weeks I was worrying that he could take me home.

And you worry about that?

[Silence]

I was in bed last night thinking about all the things that you have done in your lifetime. You were an administrator at Grafton, the Children's Home, Sisters of Mercy, Baggot Street; you were a teacher and principal in schools throughout the diocese; you also did training with personality profiling– PRH–do you remember that one?

No. What was that?

It was a type of personal development programme.

Oh I wasn't in that I was younger to know that. My biggest thing I feel is the kids.

At St Joseph's?

No you probably don't know. Ah ah they're women and they ah they um bring meaning into their lives to get to be a supportive person and two of them are in this here I can say to Emmie E. and I can say good morning Amanda A. how are you and so to so to Emmie E. hello and she'd grunt. And she is beautiful and that is where she came to when she too into here. She is a darling.

When did this happen?

187

This happened when I was in down in what way to go. We go down down down...

Sydney?

No, not that far.

Well we are in Casino now.

No, no

Where do you think you are now?

No idea... I was sick. No I was hurt. I what happened to me. There were two sisters and I didn't know why I was one of them... yesterday.

It feels like yesterday?

No. I hadn't known that one of those girls is me.

Oh! I'm a bit slow aren't I?

I'm slow. Anyway M. I know she is her name and the other one is me.

There you go.

Anyway ah ah my sister um how did I get those kids into this. M. ...

So, what you are saying is that of all the ministries that you had during your religious career...

Mm-hmm!

... the one that touched you the most and meant the most to you was the one where you were working with children?

Yes.

So what exactly was it that you did for the children that made you feel it so much?

Well this is the biggest one. M., no not M.!

You do not have to tell me the names, just tell me what you did that made it meaningful for you.

I could get somebody to go out and get these kids... protector's kids and that is it.

So you felt like you were a protector of the children and that was your main job. So that they could grow up and have a chance in life?

Yes. And um the um yeah there is two of them...

I think your glasses need cleaning.

[Laughter]

Um what was the question?

The question was: out of all the ministries that you did during your time, which one meant the most to you, and you said the children and that was because you were able to protect them and help them to achieve their potential when they grew up.

188

Well the last lot the second the last one they are ladies...
And they have done wonderful things with their lives?
Yes and they were kids who had no one for them.
To look after them and care for them?
No. My sister... wait a minute... my um sister D. had a a um brother who ate not ate she had a woman a woman who was I don't know she does because people got in on it. She was the from there to there to anyway. She was ringing. Getting on... I don't know how to say the word!
I don't know what you are talking about either and don't you dare do that. Put it here.
[Laughter]
What would you say?
She was there and it was ringing...
Yeah! Yes.
The telephone? The mobile phone?
No. The...
The house?
The drink!
The drink was ringing?
The drink!
Was there ice in it or something?
No. She never had her she was getting into her mouth into morning every day.
Oh! She was an alcoholic. Dong!!! Give the woman a prize.
[Laughter]
It is like playing charades with you sometimes.
[Laughter]
Now wait a minute that is right. She would glug, glug, glug, glug.
Did she have any alcohol brain damage?
No. But she had a no... She didn't have any children because no one would help her. Anyway my most beautiful girl who was one of my was a lady what's her name she also has dementia and she got a he is a nice kind of man ah... now I was down in... halfway down the line my it was she was a lovely lady...
That would have to be... wouldn't it?
No.
[Laughter and hand clapping in amusement at the joke]
I just wanted to catch you off guard and see what you would do.
She was lovely.
You are dementing girl!
[Laughter]

Anyway I had to. I don't know actually why I had to be in down in the line and she was in hospital for some time. I couldn't find out why I wasn't in hospital I didn't bother about it and that what that but um ...

Okay I went down to this place where the mother had placed out no she wasn't putting away but the mother kept her but I worried about the trouble and everybody worried about where the money was going and where anyway this one came to a good end actually I don't know who topped the fathers time because at the moment he is in prison he goes up to on his this is great because I when I wanted one of the kids go over where what do ya call it the the the up behind us have you ever sat here ad hear a ...

There is an aerodrome just over there.

Yes, yes. Well he was one of the things ...

Is this your nephew?

This is one of the one of the ones that kids ...

You helped him too.

We are going to go off the kids now.

Yeah.

You used to run courses that helped people know themselves.

Yeah, yeah.

What were those courses called?

These children ...

No, not the children. Let's go off the children for a while.

What?

I want you to talk about the courses in the personalities. Working with people and helping them ...

Oh yes.

... figure out what their personality was and stuff like that.

It was my love.

Yes, you loved doing it.

And, and ...

I can't remember what the name of it was Mary. My memory is going.

Is she the same?

She has gone to God.

But when she was in the beginning.

She never demented no. She was very unwell physically, but she never lost her memory.

Yeah. Yeah. She was the one I lost.

Lost! What do you mean you lost her?

Most people come to me to say hello Mary how are you and she didn't. She was there but she didn't.
She didn't come to you?
Well she might have known she knew me or something or rather but I can remember of her saying thank you and left me.
So you think that you had some kind of argument?
No, no, no, no, no.
You just didn't get along well?
No.
I wonder why as you are two highly intelligent women.
I don't know when you get up to this woman. When I um the noises coming out there over my thinking it might reach it easier here and one day it might come to you it went and it might come back and its.

Mary reminisced about her nephew.

I don't know where I am?
In what sense Mary?
I don't know any more.
You don't know any more?
Now why do you say that?
Because that is what I thought you said and I was just repeating it. You didn't say that?
What was that?
You don't know any more.
No right yeah. I haven't got any money.
What would you do with the money?
I don't know. Oh dear. I'm bad about that.
About what?
Don't know any betty any mess any … Oh I'm in here but I don't want to be in here.
Where would you want to be?
In the next life.
You want to be in the next life?
Yeah. No no um this is …
For people with dementia?
Is that what here is?
Where you are is a unit for people with dementia.
Oh great! Are you?
[Laughter]

Mary, I hate to have to tell you this but I am just a visitor.
[Laughter]
That is great because to get one around you is wonderful.
The problem is Mary, I can leave but you cannot.
I can!
No you can't.
Why?
Because this is a locked dementia unit.
What for?
Because they do not want people to be running off.
Am I still in the convent?
No you are in Casino in a locked dementia ward.
Are you?
No, you!
[Laughter]
As I said I am only a visitor.
Oh you.
[Laughter]
How does that make you feel being in a locked ward?
Oh God.
I could say 'yes my daughter.'
Where did you get the ...
[Laughter]
Who is the patient and who is the visitor here!

When do you go?
I don't know.
You have to stay.
I have to stay!
What's that?
It's the tape recorder that I am using to tape our conversations with.
Oh right.
For the book.
How are they going?
Up to about page 85. It's very hard reading.
Is it?
I've got to clean it up. I am only just transcribing it at the moment.
Okay.

Where are you going?

I am going home to Kempsey.
Are you truly? You are in Kempsey aren't you? Do you like living in Kempsey?
I think Kempsey is the best place in the world to live.
Truly?
Yep!
I take it on God not here please.
Well it wouldn't matter whether you were here or in Kempsey Mary because you are in a locked dementia ward.
Why did that happen?
Ah because when you first came here you were able to walk around and they didn't want you to wander away from the building because you might not remember.
Oh I didn't know that.
Yeah, when you were in Grafton you were having a few difficulties and they thought that this was the best place for you. I don't think they had a locked dementia bed in Grafton at that time.
Why would they not tell me?
I think that they did and I think that you have forgotten.
Oh! Of course!! [Mary said this in a very droll, dry tone.]
[Laughter]
I hope that tone is targeted at someone else 'cause if it is not, I am going to pull your nose. No, we have had this conversation several times Mary and every time you say 'but nobody has told me' and …
You keep saying that I've told you?
No, other people have told you and I've told you yeah. It is hard because that is what dementia is about.
Oh dementia! I know dementia is here.
A lot of the time!
[Mary poked her tongue out and started blowing raspberries.]
But sometimes I am good!
Sometimes you are good. Sometimes I ask you questions and you are very articulate. At the moment, this is the most articulate you have been, or should I say, the most awake you have been for three or four visits.
Well get me a coat and I will lie on the florn!
Get me a coat and I will lie on the florn?
[Silence]

Hello. Is there anybody home?
I don't know. There is a whole lot of stuff along there. I don't know whether it's …
I think one of the things I have noticed in this time is there appears to be

some personality changes.
What is that?
In that you are not–don't seem to be yourself. Although you are really upbeat and enjoying yourself, there just appear to be some differences that I do not quite understand. It doesn't seem to be you, to me. I can't explain it any better than that.
What are you not looking at?
What am I not looking at?
Mm-hmm!
Well, I am looking at you. I'm not looking at anybody else. Do you think I am not telling you the truth?
No, no. I'd never do that!
How good 'cause I am not telling the truth.
[There is silence for a short period, then Mary jokingly shapes up to hit me]

Is that right? Are you telling me the truth?
Yes, oh God yes. I am telling you the truth. I just think there appears to be some kind of personality change at the moment. For example, the way you were talking about the nurse earlier on. I have never heard you talk about a person like that in the past.
In the park?
Definitely not in a park. In the past.
Oh the past.

This is a house here. That is where the people are. I went to here where ah the place. In there there is a place..
It is the dining room in the dementia wing.
I went from ah Grafton with kids ah very um good kids people who were going into bigger bigger bigger... The kids are going through again it reminded me of well one thing that happened I had my head when I came into that room and come into school there and got everything.
You've only lost your memory in the last two or three years Mary.
Yeah.
For the first 80 years you were a most articulate and intelligent woman.
Yeah. Yeah.
This is part of your illness. One day they will be able to cure it.
Yeah. What stage am I in?
[Sigh] Well if you asked me a month ago I would have said that you were in the end stage.
What is that?

Meaning that you were going to die soon.
What's that?
Meaning you were going to God.
[Mary made a noise simulating shock]
Oh!
[Laugh]
You don't have to look so damn happy about it!
I am. I am.
Why are you happy about going to God?
I like it. God is there waiting for me.
God will be waiting for you, yes. The absolute look of happiness on your face was amazing. You deserve it. So, if I said that you were going to God in the morning, you would get up and dance?
[Mary clapped her hands]
And Mary came out to meet me.
And Mary came out to meet me!
People forget that Mary is the Mother.
I think that men forget that Mary is the Mother! And men forget that the church would not be as strong as it is without the women…
Yes.
And Mary is the foundation of the Church, not just Peter.
Well the thing is that what is in the Church what is in my round is ah when I had that thing way down there I did I came we were when Ilene that happened and others died there were others that came to see me and look after me and um I don't know if they came to see me I had not mother, no dad, no Ilene and I felt that very much…
[Mary broke down in tears]
It is okay to cry Mary.
And I came out to how would I do this and it came out in my helping for the children and that is what I went what did I come to in here. I didn't come into that I don't know what I come into…
You haven't come into here for Ministry, Mary. You have come into here to be ministered to.
When?
In here as a patient.
I don't look after the people in here?
No, you don't. You've come in here to be looked after. Okay! You have done your job…
That right. That's right. I've talked about that I've gone to no, no it's over for me and I am going to have to and listen to what is happening for me.

195

Exactly.

Hmm?

Exactly. It is over for you. It is your time to rest...

Yeah.

... and let others be there for you.

Yes.

Let's go back to when I said that I thought a month ago you were going to go to God and you got really excited about that. You said that God would be there waiting for you but that Mary would come to meet you. You talked about Mary being forgotten within the Church–what do you think that Mary would say once she came to meet you in heaven?

Jesus I would say. What do you think?

You would say Jesus?

Yes.

Just Jesus?

Yes.

What does that mean to you?

Well death and what's his name, Jesus was a man and he um to me he doesn't big up in the man there all God and everything else.

He is humble you mean?

Something like that and this is out of the what but forget it it's not I'm God and Jesus, I'm do you have an interest in what's his name...

Jesus?

No.

God?

No. Besides that is that man what's his name? N.... I cannot handle that fellow's name but I want to get out on him. I don't want him to get out of. I want to know who he is.

You mean the nurse?

Yes.

And I think you need to get away from me.

Why are you going to bite me or something?

No. What would be the pinch? You think I am no good?

I think you are wicked.

Oh!

Come on, you've got a good comeback. Come on that mind is gonna work in a minute and it is spit out something or are you gonna lift up that left arm and smack me.

[Laughter]

Not there anyway. Ah I don't know but I don't know I don't want to be running around making beds or doing that and I am not working.

Mary you are here because you are unwell and you are now at rest.

Where?

You are now at rest?

Why?

Because it is time for you to rest. And it is time for you to go home to God when your body is ready to go.

Yeah.

So when your body is ready to give up, you are going to close your eyes and say 'well you're ready, I'm here. Let's get the ball rolling.'

Who?

You.

[Laughter]

I don't even know the size of this place.

It is quite large. Bigger that when the Sisters were running it.

Yeah.

I think it is over 100 beds now.

Well I am not working.

You too tired to work?

No.

Yes you are.

Why?

Because you cannot even walk.

That is not work.

Walking is work for me these days.

Ah dear I wish you could stay.

I wish I could. I'll be back before Christmas.

I wonder if there will be any people around for me.

People do come and visit you Mary.

Oh I know that. People have been so lovely with me.

So what are you saying then? You want someone for you, just for you.

No. I would very gladly to see ... but and that would be good.

And I say to you Mary, that if you have to go to God before I get back, go with grace and go in peace because you have done your job, good and faithful servant.

19th December 2015

Mary, sorry I am just going to put the pillow under your shoulder.
Who are you?
Look at me. Look at me honey.
I can't. I can't...
Where are your glasses? I am from Kempsey
Oh.
Do you know who I am?
Yeah. Um!
You look like you are having a rough trot?
No I'm alright. I've got a lot.
You've got a lot?
Yes.
You've got a lot of what?
Nice things. I thought you had died.
[Laughter]
Nope. I am still here my friend.

I want to get out of, out of ... you don't see it really. Ah that is what I want.
You want a tissue?
Yes.
That is a sheet. I will find you a tissue.

Are you really … are you really …
Am I really here?
No. Are you really, really here?
Yes I am really here.
That's good.
I am not a figment of your imagination today.
[Laughter]
Yes, I still have the warped sense of humour. You are looking pretty poor, actually.
Why? What do I look like?
Um. You look exhausted. You look like you have had enough.
Well would you like to carry and have a left?
Would I like to go and have a left? What does that mean?
Yeha well, I've I've got a quiet life and you might like not …
I have no idea what you are talking about.

Truly I can tell you how to do things. This has gone on for a long time here.
I've got trying to get around into some place to fix things. I've got all sorts of things out of place. Truly.
What do you mean by all sorts of things out of place?
Ah there is a lot things that don't get to me.
People don't tell you things?
Mm-hmm.
And you miss out on information?
No. No.
Just relax.
I got down this morning, no the next day and I thought I sure I sure … and I checked and checked and checked and checked and I think she is a lady who is in the kids area and she screeps and she screeps and she screeps and she screeps …
Stop. What does screeps mean? Do you mean that she scrapes her finger nails down a blackboard?
Mm-hmm
That is a new word on me. And she irritates the hell out of you?
Yes and the she the she and she screeps as well … aha aha aha …
[Laughter]
She sounds like a demented bird.
[Laughter]
She could be.

Who am I?
Oh. The best wo wo … The best woman in the world.
[Laughter]
You are a charmer.

Now, do you remember who I am besides being 'the best woman in the world'?
Why?
I don't know. That is what you said about me.
Where did you find that?
I don't know.
Who … um you know the children they are women. People are Ettie he was she's gone.
Where has she gone?
Towards somebody whatever she was marrying a one stage I haven't got time to go looking up so!

Do you know that I love you?
I do know that you love me.
Is there any [Laugh] … this is dreadful … is there any more excuse me, no more more ah …
Chocolate?
Yeah. You know that I am cold and you say that it is very hot outside.
You are chilly.

I cover Mary with a blanket.

Is that better?
Thank you.

So, feel like going to heaven today?
No.
Good. Do you feel as if you are going any time soon?
No.
Okay. Would it be good?
No. Because if you go out of it ahm and don't come back you'll have a ah it's when you um when go to God you … ah …
That is the end of your life?
That's that's what you do but you never come back.
You don't believe in reincarnation?
[Silence]

Do you know...
Yes.
But you don't believe in it?
I don't know. I've never got into it.
Um... I think that there has to be some kind of reincarnation even though that is not a Catholic thing. I think our lives are too short to learn enough... to learn what we are supposed to learn while we are on the face of the earth...
Mm-hmm.
... and that we get various goes at it to try and learn what we need to and become better people.
Who says that?
I says that. That is my belief.
But it does come back...
Yes, we do come back. Even though there is heaven and there is God...
Yeah.
... and that we... It is sort of like a holiday for me. That is what my belief is–that heaven is a holiday while I am waiting to come back down to have another go to try and get it right again. And only until we learn what we need to learn on this earth, do we stay in heaven forever... or go onto the next cycle in our existence. Whatever that existence is!

Your eyes are crossed and you are looking rather cranky at me.
[Laughter]
I am. My eyes...
I start singing–"My eyes are crossed I cannot see, I love you because you're you..." Maybe I should be in that bed!
[Laughter]

What do you think of that statement about reincarnation?
I, I would believe it.
It is an interesting concept. Everybody has their own ideas about what happens after we go to God the first time. I don't know how long we stay in heaven after one life. It might be only a short time. Or it might be hundreds of years. Who knows!
Mm-hmm!
But I do believe that we keep on recycling back to earth until we get it right. And me, I am so slow I'll be recycling back for eternity!
[Laughter]
I love you.

201

That is good. I love you too.

I like that chocolate too!
I'll get you one.
You should be stopping me.
Why? Do you enjoy chocolate?
Yes!
So why should I be stopping you? What's it gonna do, kill ya?
No.
There you go. If you wanted a cigarette I would go out and get you one.
Do you still ...
No.
I never did.

Is your mother still alive?
No. You shot her, remember?
Yes. Oh yes.
My God ...
[Laughter]
... I could say anything that you have done and with the dementia you would agree. Did you hear what I said?
Yes.
What did I say?
[Silence]
You asked me was Mum still alive. I said, no you shot her don't you remember that. You said, yes I do remember that.
[Laughter]
So I'll take this recorder to the police and say that I have a confession here that says this woman shot another woman. Do you wish to hit me now? You think I am really strange, don't you?
Yes I do!
I've confused you haven't I?
Oh no one could be confoed about you.
[Laughter]
Yes, everyone gets confused about the words that come out of my mouth.

[I started singing] 'Jesus Christ Superstar, riding around on your Yamaha'.
Your what? Your what?
[Laughter]
Your Yamaha. It is a motorbike.

202

Oh.
Could you imagine Jesus Christ riding around on a motor bike?
You mean that you do that?
No. I'm just being a dummy.

What is that on your face?
I think it is age spots.
Really!
Oh, I don't know. I don't look at myself in the mirror much—only to comb my hair and the last time I did that was about 2013.
Is it curly?
If I let it grow it is curly. But my hair gets so thick if I let it grow that it gets really hot.
I think it is lovely.
Thank you. I'll have to cut it off then.
You're not gonna do do that.
[Laughter]
You sound so much like one of my Aunties when I say that. She hates it when I cut my hair short.

[Unintelligible] ... and I done it every time I did.
There you go.
It is amazing really.
What didn't you do? I am not really sure what you are saying.
I have never in my mind put that ... in and I think it is the first time I have ever done it.
The first time you have experienced it?
Yeah!
Well that is something amazing. 82 years and you've experienced something for the first time.
82?
Yeah. How old do you think you are?
84.
You hold your age well.
[Laughter]

Have a sip ... why thank you Sr Mary Magdalene Quinn. Do I sound facetious?
Wasn't too hard!
Snort. So you died and went to heaven. Everybody ...

Was happy!

[Laughter]

What made you say that Mary? Oh dear, I nearly choked on the laughter.

Well I tried to get my not at not my something out of it is going on.

So, lets…

[Laughter]

… go back to the story: you died and went to heaven and everybody was very sad at the funeral and you get to heaven and there is God and there is Mary standing beside him and Mary comes over to greet you. What do you think Mary would say to you?

Ah Mary. You're beautiful. You've looked after me so well.

It is obviously a beautiful image as you have a beautiful smile with a serene look on you face.

Mm-hmm!

Yes?

Yes. My mother taught me.

What did your mother teach you?

To be … to be ah well she was a very good mother until she died which was very very sad … she was so lovely and … Dad was um he could be nice to everybody and I know but I can hardly put it in my head only I cannot go and see it but there is a hospital in this is way over it is not something that runs around in Grafton. It was a … Is there a hospital?

There is a hospital over near the Children's Home.

Yes. And my Dad died there.

I had a bit of my memory on Dad when they he went into that hospital.

What do you mean a bit of your memory? You can remember some of what happened in the hospital?

Yes.

And you can't remember other bits?

Um no. Yes and no. There was a lady who was one of our nuns um who um went into the hospital. In some ways I half think that he … someone … [unintelligible].

So why did they come into the hospital if your mum and dad were dead. Who was this person visiting in hospital?

Yes not that no no.

So, what are you thinking now?

[Silence]

Mary, what are you thinking?

Who it was who …
Was in the hospital?
Yes. Where Dad … that's interesting.
What is interesting?
Huh?
Why is it interesting?
Why? What do you think?
I don't know Mary. I'm just trying to get a handle on the conversation.
Mm-hmm!

Do you know that it is Christmas in a few days?
Yes.
What are you going to do for Christmas?
I'm ahm I don't know what I could do about that.
Yeah. [I start singing Mary a Christmas song]
Hey that looks like what you were saying it goes to they do do that.
Do do what?
God can come back again.
Reincarnation?
Mm-hmm!
So you think that you will be reincarnated?
Mm-hmm!
So what would you do if you came back, if you were reincarnated after you had a bit of a break in heaven … you've done a pretty good job on earth during this reincarnation Mary Magdalene Quinn. What would you like to do during your next reincarnation?
Um! Doing what I do what I've done now.
You would like to be a sister?
Mm-hmm!
The sisters as a religious entity may have packed it in by the time you were reincarnated. How does that make you feel?
Oh it's not a big oh come here and do that …
You think that is okay because God will find another way for you to minister to his people?
Ah. I've never thought of it. I'm not interested in one way.
Because you are not going to be around?
Mm-hmm!
So it doesn't matter what happens?
[Silence]

If you could be anybody on the face of this earth either living or dead, who would you want to be?

You.

Why me?

You've been so kind and I'm not the only one and I get another lot of chocolate.

[Laughter]

Hilarious! I was about to say that I am touched Mary. So let's be serious now, if you could be anybody, either living or dead, who would you be— besides me because I am bringing you more chocolate?

You know the thing that as on the other side of the middle of the road there is a lady over there?

On the other side of the road that is J. and M.

Something ... anyway I can't go any further in that sort of sense.

On the news this morning Mother Theresa's second miracle has been agreed to and they are going to make her a saint.

What?

To become a saint in the Church you have to have performed two verified miracles. I don't know what she did but they reckon they are miracles. As far as I'm concerned she doesn't need any blokes from the Church saying that she is a saint, she was probably one when she was born.

What?

And I bet that she doesn't have to reincarnate!

Oh!

You are a bit confused?

Yes.

I think we will let this one go.

What was it like living in the time of the Second Vatican Council? Do you remember it?

What?

Do you remember the Second Vatican Council back in 1964, starting with Pope John and finishing with Pope Paul? A lot of things changed within the church.

You're very able to do things that I don't in my mind.

But you can't in your mind?

No.

Do you know that after you got sick you lost a lot of memory because of the illness? How does that make you feel?

It is not the illness. Is that an ass...

[Laughter]

Sorry...

[Laughter]

Sorry... What happened to me...

You've got dementia.

Is that a sickness?

Yes. What did you think it was? It is part of your body that is not working properly. Like say cancer in some part of the body: that part of the body that has cancer is not working properly.

Ah!

So yes, you are sick.

Oh!

What did you think it was?

I knew that it was something that changed you.

Do you feel changed?

No no... yes, yes, yes I feel very angry that I changed it.

That you changed it or your body did?

I did.

How can you change your illness?

My what?

How can you change so that you become ill? Or what did you change?

[Silence]

Yes the dementia is an illness.

I didn't know that. What does my part of being that how do you come to its sickness?

It is a sickness that cannot yet be healed.

I think I'm pretty much set in.

You've pretty much forgotten everything—is that what you are saying?

No. Oh I don't know!

Does it frustrate you that you sometimes can't start or finish a conversation well?

Well it comes to me as um people take away what I can do. Anyway...

It comes to me that people can take away what I can do. People are not taking away what you can do. Your body is doing that Mary.

Say that again.

Your body is taking away what you can do or what you used to do. It is not someone taking it away from you; it is your body being ill. Do you understand that?

207

Ah yes but I um there is something that I um you're not [unintelligible]...deminya...dementia um...takes things away from what I could do. Is that what I said?

Yes, the dementia is taking things away from what you could do or what you used to do. You find it very difficult to have a conversation or remember things.

I ah there the other day and I was grateful for this that I um um I um was happy about it, I was satisfied because it is going to happen and um ah because I can't um the sister I spoke to about it what why I thought to myself, who did the doing of my being to what I had to probably I had what I wanted to have.

Meaning you had a good life?

[Silence]

You said what you wanted to have, and I am not sure what you wanted to have?

No. I was getting old somebody I remembered quite okay about it that um I have this thing that I'm not going to get it. I don't have to sort of let it off and I nearly when I after...

So, you didn't think that you were going to get dementia as you were getting older and now you've got it and that made you very angry?

No. For me I just put up my um and ah I wasn't I'm not being responsible for what um it's not me.

What is happening now is not you?

Yes!

So if it is not you, who is it?

[Silence]

Sorry Mary. No one can answer that. It is one of the unanswerable questions. What is happening is the dementia is taking you away from who you are.

So, what you said: if you are not you, okay, the dementia is taking your personality away. Is that what you are saying?

No!

So what is the dementia taking away?

Um...

The dementia is taking away who you are?

Yes.

Does that make you sad? Or are you just accepting that this is part of the illness?

I think so. As you've said a couple of times I said that um what I need to do is um what is it, I didn't care to something that I can't go into and that's doesn't ah hold me um I've had my time and I have my friends; I haven't my mum; I haven't my dad; I haven't a number of things but I'm satisfied with what is there and what's there is there and it is pretty good.

I think you are an amazing lady Mary Quinn.

I can still think. That is good.

What do you think about?

I know that I um ahm I can get into my place at…I think I can get in what I want at least. I go back to the sisters said…in some ways something is knocked off um…

[Silence for long period]

Do you think a lot about God?

Do I what?

Do you think a lot about God?

No.

Do you think a lot about what you used to?

I can't.

Why can't you?

Because um the lady came and said ah you I think she said I don't have the same pottery that I had and that was fine. It came to that I gone to the not what I can do now it actually gave me a freedom and if I have a freedom I'm heading for God. I don't help anybody here who can do something. I know God will look after me.*

God is here.

[Silence for long period].

*Although this is primarily a chronicle of Mary's journey into her illness, it is also about Mary and her faith as they cannot be separated. This is why I feel compelled to comment on the above statement made by Mary.

The analogy of the potter, the clay and the potter's wheel is a fairly famous biblical story. For those who don't know the story it is basically about each one of us being clay moulded and shaped at the potter's wheel–with the potter being God and the wheel being life.

I cannot presume to faithfully interpret what Mary said but I am going to convey what I believe. I interpret Mary's choice of the word 'pottery' as being the clay–that she being the clay had changed in some fundamental way because of her illness. She knows, understands and accepts this–and according to Mary this has brought her freedom.

A non-religious–or perhaps even a religious–person may view these words by Mary as the hallucinatory ramblings of an ill woman. As a fully paid-up member of the 'doubting-Thomas Society', had I not been there to hear her words and how she said them, I might have said 'yeah just another ramble along the crumbling pathways of Mary's mind'. It doesn't matter what I, or whoever reads this passage, thinks because I believe that Mary experienced something very special at this time.

In my is um there is a lot … what was I gonna say something about a cat …
[Laughter]
I have no idea about what you were trying to say Mary. I've never seen you with a cat.
No. I um just let it go. Let it go. Let it go. Let it go. Let it go.
Does that frustrate you when you can't think about what you want to say?
Mm-hmm. Sigh!

You were saying earlier …
Yeah! What?
That you felt freedom. Do you remember saying that?
The what?
You felt free.
Yes.
Can you explain that to me a little bit more?
Um. I have a feeling that is um better. I have there is something that I can't I am able to get me a place where I … had just before I spoke that this morning I thought um I what I have a gad … for me but um that has a very please pleasing me um … there is a … I hope you are not finished.
No I am still here sitting and listening and waiting for you. Just enjoying the silence and enjoying your company.

[Silence for some time]
Oh dear.
What is wrong?
I get the … I don't know. I don't know what it is. It is something that I'm be in the bottom and not instead of a good thing … Is it right to sit on your bottom?
You mean on a chair, on the floor or on the bed?
On the bed.

It is okay to sit anywhere on your bottom that is comfortable for you Mary.
Is that what you are asking?
No. There is um get at not on right.
Is your bottom sore?
It is not good at the minute.
I could shoot you and put you out of your misery.
Oh you could ... oh it has gone out of my head!
Damn!
Yeah.

What are you thinking or are you sleeping?
Eh!
What are you thinking or are you sleeping?
No I'm not. I'm trying to work out this um this ah ... what are you saying?
It is not me. It is a lady walking past.
[Period of silence]

So what are you thinking about now?
Wondering what you are thinking.
Ahm. I'm thinking why ... I'm thinking that it is an interesting place that we are both in. That I am here sitting beside you in a nursing home in a dementia unit in Casino. If someone had asked me where I think I would be at this time 20 or 30 years ago I don't think I would ever have envisaged this.
Having?
Having envisaged this.
What?
I would never have believed that this was possible. That you would be here in a chair not being able to walk and not being able to care for yourself and your dementia is making it difficult for you to communicate. And me here being on a walking stick. I would never have guessed that's where we would be at this time. I am just thinking that life has a lot of challenges for all of us.
Mm-hmm.
And you know I am not that healthy myself. And you, your trouble with the dementia—life always throws challenges at us. I suppose that is what I am thinking ...
Mm-hmm.
... and then you come along and you talk about what God is for you and how you feel freedom at times and you throw away a sentence that is absolutely

mind-blowing—it has come through your soul and I think that an amazing thing that even though you have dementia, we can still communicate with each other. So that was what I was thinking.
Ah ha.
Was that a good enough thought?
Yeah.
Yeah. And I was also thinking that geez it would be good if I could go to bed and lie down.
Well why don't you do it?
I'll go very shortly.

Can you see the clouds and sky outside?
Where? Oh yes yeah!
What does it feel like to be looking at them and to know that you will never walk out in the sun again with the wind on your face or to walk along the beach and feel the sand under your feet?
I don't think any of those is I can say yes yes yes yes. I can't. Yes.
Is it sad? Does it make you sad? Or is it just the reality that your body is the way it is and you are accepting of that.
Yes. Yep. Oh you poor old thing.
[Laughter]

May the Lord keep you, may the Lord shine his face upon you and you shall be whatever you need to be.
Amen.
Amen.
You're a little ...
Pain in the neck?
... a little girl ... come back here and look at me ... go back and you come ...
How could I have been such a naughty child and to have grown up into wonderful adult—is that what you are thinking?
No!
[Laughter]
Okay.
[Laughter]

20th December 2015

I remember ages ago…
That you used to throw chalk at me.
[Laughter]
You wanna hit me now?
Nope. But I love to love you.
I love to love you too.

We should give you KFC every day.
Why?
Because you would eat the food then. But then again, you would get used to it.

Something happened.
What do you mean?
I got something somebody put a note on the floor over home and my sister Ilene I forgot. Isn't that amazing?
You forgot that Ilene had died?
No!!! I no…
You saw Ilene after this note was dropped on the floor?
No the note there was a note.
And it was from Ilene?
Mm-hmm.

She sent you a note from heaven saying why in the hell weren't you there yet!
[Laughter]
Sorry. What did the note say?
I don't know what I did but Ilene was am I think she was ...

We were disturbed by one of the other residents.

Now where was I?
Ilene dropped a note on the floor.

We were then disturbed by the nursing staff.

I wish I could find the sisters from in our M. I think there are eight of them still here.
Eight who? Sisters?
Mm-hmm.
Here in St Michaels?
Here yes in St. Michaels.

Okay my maths is pretty poor. What is two plus two?
What do you mean?
What is the answer when you add two and two?
Why?
I just want to know if you remember your math. So, if two plus two is four, what is two plus three?
I don't know.
Mm-hmm. How does that make you feel?
What?
That you can't do simple maths anymore.
What did you say? What did you say?
I said, if two plus two is four, what is two plus three?
Um, there um I don't know I don't get any place then that is fair enough. It's not me.
No, it is not you any more, is it!

Do they say it is over?
Is what over?
With you.
It is over?
No more!
Shoot me and put me out of my misery?

No. Have...
There is still more chicken here. Here is a bit.
Thank you. Could I make a question about our bodies?
Yes.
My body.
Yes, your body.
Um do um...

Long period of silence while eating KFC.

Mary then went off onto a long mumbled dialogue about Cowper and Maclean that I was unable to transcribe.

Mary when you are telling me all about this, about Cowper and the schools in Maclean and the sisters, are you seeing a visualisation of that in your mind? Are you seeing the memory of it in pictures in your mind?
Yes.
You can see it?
Yes. Yes.
You can't get the words out well enough. Is that it?
Yes.
It is just really interesting watching you. You have been talking solidly now for about five minutes and you seem to be looking at something while you are talking. You can't seem to get the words out real well but...
No.
... but you know what you are trying to say and well you actually look like you are looking at a picture.
Ah!
I was wondering if the memory was in your mind and were you looking at the memory.
Yes. Well the sisters ah I dad went off took um it wasn't us us in the we had about six kids now I know Ilene Ilene is I tell you did I say to you that I told you um... It's gone.
Damn!
Yeah. I'll hit your head and you can hit mine.
[Laughter]
Okay one, two, three, slap!
[Laughter]
Oh that was funny. It is awful when your brain doesn't work well.
Yeah. Also as an other...

We were disturbed by another resident.

Yesterday you were talking about going to heaven and having a good long break. I was talking too about what I felt reincarnation was and that I believed in reincarnation–that we came back to earth until we basically got it right as human beings; until we become, you know, really good people. I asked you if you believed in reincarnation and you said that you hadn't thought about it before. Reincarnation is not part of the Catholic faith as we know it. So what do you think of reincarnation?
[Silence]
Do you think it is a possibility?
Well that is like um that.
That is like that. I am not sure I understand what that means Mary?
No.
Is it too hard for you to think about?
I think, see um ah ...
I know you are thinking because you are frowning.
[Silence]
Oh you are not thinking 'cause you are not frowning anymore.
[Laughter]

I started singing the Christmas song 'Mary's Boy Child'.

Hey, hey, hey.
Hey what?
It says and they will live for evermore because of Christmas day.
So Jesus died and he reincarnated. So if Jesus reincarnated, doesn't it also mean that we reincarnate?
Mm-hmm! Mm-hmm!
But I think that the Catholic Church believes that we reincarnate only once. I hope that we get to have a good sleep so that I can have a good rest.
Get onto the girls.
Get onto the girls. Which ones?
[Laughter]
Excuse me, we've got one coming up who is a bit cranky and she would like to have a good long rest. Can you tell St Peter to meet her at the gate and knock her on the head with a piece of 4x2.
[Laughter]
They won't know what hit 'em when we turn up.
Yes.

'And we will live for evermore because of Christmas day.' So what does that really mean? I actually believe that we reincarnate more than once and that

we keep on coming back so that we can look at the mistakes we have made in previous lives.

I sang parts of Noel.

I really admire some of the singers.
Your singing?
No. I'm not really keen on my singing, that is for sure. I admire the singing of those with beautiful voices.

Mary Quinn, what is two plus two?
Fifteen.
[Laughter]
One plus one.
[Silence]
You appear to have completely have lost the concept.
What?
You have completely lost the concept of mathematics.
Why?
Because you cannot do the simplest of sums, like addition.
[Disdainful laugh]
You don't believe me?
No. Yes.
You can't have it both ways.
No. Not God.
What do you mean by not God?
I don't know.
Interesting.
Not God.
It might be God. He might have taken your ability to understand the concept. It appears to be completely foreign to you. You don't appear to understand. I asked you a very simple maths question—like what is two plus two—and you do not understand the question.
[Silence]
Hello. Is there anybody home?
Yes. Two. No four.
Oh my. Well done. So you do understand it when you think about it. Amazing. Is that because you got cranky 'cause you couldn't remember?
No.
You just thought about it for a little while?

Um I think you wanted to get out of here.
You want me to leave?
No I want you to have your way.
Have my way. If it's okay I will stay for a little while longer.
[Silence for some time]

What do you think your quality of life is like Mary?
Beg your pardon?
What do you think your quality of life is like? You are losing your memory. You can't care for yourself anymore. You cannot walk. People have got to feed you and dress you.
Ohhhhhhhh! Wait about. Wait about.
That is the reality. You cannot walk. You cannot dress.
I can.
Who put your dress on you this morning?
Yeah.
The nurses.
[Mary put on an act of pretending to cry and then burst into laughter.]
Oh you are a card.
[Silence]

Do you feel that your quality of life is pretty poor?
What about you?
I can actually still walk. I can actually still think for myself. My body is falling apart, I agree, but I can still basically care for myself. Whereas you are unable to care for yourself. Does this make you angry?
No it doesn't it doesn't it's not the fact that I don't get um I'm not able its people keeping on me because they want to keep me alive.
You don't want to be alive?
I do! I do!
Why do you want to be alive? I know that it is a human thing to want to be alive, but I've known of people in your situation who would rather say 'I have had enough let me go'.
I wouldn't do that.
I know. I think it is the Catholic in you.
Um well it's not. It's keep away or something.
I know that if I was in your position, I wouldn't want to be here.
Yeah!
To be disabled as you are, no, I wouldn't wish to struggle with that. But yesterday when we were talking, you said that you could 'still think'. So you

are lying in that chair and you are actually doing something. So your brain is still working to a certain degree. Do you agree?
I don't know. Wadda ya is that a somebody got a time up ...

I have never asked ...
What?
I didn't have to ask something because um it wasn't necessary.
I don't understand?
The others keep asking me or doing handover I'm in one sense I'm a bit of the follow of you in me ...
In one sense you agree with me, that you do not want to be around in this condition. Is that what you are saying?
No, no not at all.
What are you thinking Mary?
There is people like you have want to ... Sometimes I have given up on it um you are saying that I can't do, I can't do well I can't do because I'd be silly if I did more. I'm hurt, I am unable I can't cook I can't, can't, can't, can't, can't. But that doesn't make that from that.
Doesn't make you less a person?
No! And there is it is what pulls me up is that other peoples does it. Not because um I didn't something because ah people want me like you bring me food and stuff and that would be.
So, what I think you are saying is I am making an assumption that your quality of life is poor—and that I should not make that assumption ...
No, no you are not doing that at all. This is a good day to make pull this up. There are people getting this um this chickens and whatever they are. I've never asked me to get it. You love me and you I would never say oh get out of the way, I don t like you. But um and there's plenty of room around where I've always lived. Mum and dad would be amazed that I would never been able to do what I do to need be in a good place. That is the way that I look at it. What do you say?
I'm not sure I totally understand. What I think you're saying is, it is okay to be where I am because this is where I am supposed to be basically ...
Yeah.
... and that I've got something to offer other people still ...
Yeah, yeah.
... by them visiting me.
Yeah.
Is that what you are saying?
Yeah.

I love you MMQ. You didn't see that, did you?

What?

I just poked my tongue out at you.

[Laughter]

Tell me what you are thinking?

What am I thinking?

Mm-hmm.

I am thinking that for someone who is suffering from dementia, you have struggled really hard to make people understand what you are trying to say—and I really appreciate that human struggle within you. To try and help me understand what you are feeling and where you are at.

Basically, I feel like you've said to me: back off—I may look like I've got nothing else to offer anybody during this last bit of my life but I believe that I have just by being here; being ill doesn't mean that I cannot still give to other people. Even if it is to kiss one of the other ladies or just to say hello to someone, you still have something to offer.

Mm-hmm!

And I find that an amazing thing, that someone who is so unwell is still ministering God's word. So I hail you Sr Mary.

You are talking about what you you see um you do look after me.

With the little bit of time that I have, I do as much as I can.

Yeah!

I think that I wake you up by coming and seeing you and having conversations with you. Actually, I don't think that you relate to anybody much unless you have visitors.

Yeah!

And a lot of people don't know how to communicate with people who have dementia. Whereas I try and engage you in conversation. Do you feel other people are uncomfortable with your illness?

No.

See that is an amazing thing too.

Actually I um there is something that two of us actually do well.

How do we do well? Besides being good mates.

Well that is a big thing.

It is. It is one of our most precious gifts to each other.

Mm-hmm! I'm looking here on a thing I'm a I'm looking at the girls who work for me over there and you look for me very much I mean I their job is Grafton Convent is for them but you um do more they do that but it is not as much um I there is a two sided thing.

um . . .
[Silence]

Lunch is here. I will leave you and see you in a month or so.
Okay.
And may the Lord be with you and protect you over the next several weeks that I am not here.
Amen.
What are you thinking? Hello!
I love, I mean thinking of the things that well just hear the girls say and we might all be dead this year.
We might. Your point?
Well we just have to have some think...
Go with the flow. You never know when your time is going to be up.
No.
And it doesn't really matter. It is the journey that is important, not the ending.
Mm-hmm!
You agree with me?
Yes I do
And in your case the ride is rather bumpy towards the end and I suppose mine is too but you gotta go somehow. We all have some kind of bumpy road to the end.

30th January 2016

Good morning.
Good morning.
How are you feeling?
Oh! Not very fusty.
Not very fusty?
Yeah. Who are you?
Who am I?
Yeah?
I'm the strangest student you ever had.
Oooooh! I new'd you'd come. I love you. I love you still.
I'm glad you do 'cause I love you too. How are you?
I've been good hands for a bad time.
You've been good hands for a bad time!
Yeah.
You've been having a bad time?
No I don't think so.
[Silence]

Your taste buds seem to have changed because I brought you the exact same chocolate last time and you absolutely loved it. This time you don't like it so much. Isn't that funny?
It is.

Maybe you will like it tomorrow?
Ah ha!

So I've been working on our book…
Have you ever given up to looking at it now?
No, I am still working on it. It is still going to be published. That is, if you want it published.
I do and I want to look at it…

We are disturbed by the nurse.

So yeah, I still want to publish the book. I have been working on the Introduction and transcribing some of what was said last time I was here.

I read some of what I had written. I wanted to see if Mary had any comment to make about it.

Did you take any of that in?
No!
I didn't think so, but I felt that I needed to read that bit out to you.
What was it? Say it again.
I'm not going to say the whole thing again.

I spoke briefly about the potter comment.

Do you remember it at all now?
No!
How does it make you feel when you cannot remember something like that?
[Silence]

What are you thinking?
Just thinking what the… what was you thinking and I haven't had time to put it together.
It is hard to put things together?
[Silence]

Are you going to sleep on me?
Say that again.
Are you going to sleep on me?
No. No.
[Silence]

So how are you feeling?
[Silence]
Hey!
I'm thinking … I …
You were thinking what?
[Laugh]
Cannot get the brain going this morning?
No but that is alright.
Just cannot get the words out?
Ah … I'm thinking … um … that I am …
Think that I am?
[Silence]
You've gone away.
I beg your pardon?
You've gone away.
What is that?
Meaning you've started a conversation and you have not finished it.
I'm away.
Are you away?
Yeah!
Okay. That was really emphatic.

So, what are you thinking?
[Silence for a period]

I cannot remember what the last thing I said was.
I don't remember either as it was so long ago.
I have made such a wonderful they …
They have been such a wonderful?
That there is so …
[Silence]

You still with me?
Yes. [Unintelligible] … I've left you.
You've left me?
Yes.
Why?
What do you mean?
You just said you've left me and I asked you why you have left me.
I haven't left you.

Good. Do you know who I am?
Yeah.
Who am I?
You.
[Laughter]
You've been very so much you've given me.
I know what you are trying to say. It is hard to get a straight sentence out these days.
Yeah.

I am wondering if I can get anything out of you. I want to ask you a question because I have been working on the…
Okay.
… Introduction to the book. I am going to call it a chronicle, more than a book, because it is about your conversations with me. As I was working on the Introduction I thought you should have a chance to say something before it goes to print. So, if you were given the chance to say anything about this chronicle of your journey into dementia, what would you like to say to people?
The dementia stuff is terrible.
The dementia stuff is terrible.
I um…
[Mary shrugged her shoulders]
… it hasn't bothered me.

Are you in dementia?
Am I in dementia?
Yeah.
No, I do not have dementia.
Yeah! Yeah!
I have memory loss occasionally. Why are you asking am I in dementia?
[Unintelligible] I don't care about it.
You don't care about dementia?
No.
It is just part of getting on with life and going to God?
Um um…

You are not pushing me at all.
[Groan]
Are you in pain?

Yeah.

Where is the pain?

Yesterday...

The pain was yesterday?

... at I oh rang hit me [unintelligible] ... Now I am going to say now what are you going to do?

I am not going to sing and put you out of your misery.

[Laughter]

I was talking about working on the Introduction to the chronicle that we are doing together and I thought that you should have an opportunity to say what you wanted to say about your journey into the dementia. What would you like to say to anybody who reads what we have written?

[Silence]

I made an imitation snore.

Oh dear!

[Silence]

No I am not.

You are not what?

I'm not I am too ... I am too ...

You are tired today?

Yeah.

Do you need to go sleep?

I don't know too weak that I don't want someone to make me ... [unintelligible] ... but sounds silly.

Did it sound silly?

No.

Are you feeling a little confused?

Yep!

Is that frustrating?

Nope. I'll see you back or are you not going to?

Where am I going back?

I'm just wondering when ...

No, I am here for another couple of hours. I can just sit here and read my book if you need to rest.

Nooo. I want you to talk to me.

Where am I sitting.

You are not sitting, you are lying in bed.

[Laughs] Lucky me.
You like lying in bed?
Yeah. Who is in bed?
You, Mary Quinn. Is there something wrong with that?
[Silence]

Where am I?
You are in your room at St Michael's in Casino.
Yeah. Yeah. Its I can't get out.
No, because you cannot walk anymore.
My legs are dreadful.
Well, we will have to get the girls to get you out of bed as soon as…
My bed.
Yeah, and give you a bit of a shower.
No, no, no. No shower today.
Why don't you want a shower today?
Because you are here.
It will only take them a short while, but if you are in pain the hot water might help your legs.
Yeah. No I can't do it. Is that what happened. You don't… if you… I think that you… You think that I?
[Silence for a long period]

What are you thinking Mary?
My the way I'm fitting if you think if you think I am I can't see…
You keep on saying 'if you think' and I am not sure you are thinking what I am thinking. Except that I think you are an amazing lady who has come through an amazing journey. Do you want me to tell you what I think?
Yes.
Okay. Well…
What?
You're hot?
You're not!
[Laughter]
I'm getting hot too. It is a very hot day outside.
Is it.
Yesterday was a rough day, weather-wise.

I'm thinking that I think if I was in your position with dementia, I don't think I could handle it with as much grace as you. You are so accepting of the fact

227

that you have dementia at this moment. I remember when you first got it, you were pretty cranky about it. But as time has gone on, you seem to have come to an accommodation with it in your life—you live with it. I think that you still believe you are one of His children and that at some point you will be coming home to Him. That is what I think. So what do you think?
[Silence]
Did you hear any of that?
No.
No! I said all these beautiful things about you and you didn't hear it. You've gone to sleep have you?
No.
Where are you then?
I'm in my supposed to be in a [unintelligible] ... I'm in the ...
You are in the bed at St Michael's.
No. I am not in a bed I am be ... I don't know what the bed is. It's got ...
Are you frustrated at the moment?
No! In the ... [Sigh!] I don't know what it is. If you don't know what I am can I don't know why the people to dent to that in they get in the too they have they ...
I can see you are really trying to get something out.
Yeah. Do you know what ahm ... I don't know. Do you know?
No, I do not know what you are trying to say Mary.
Yes. I am certainly not seeing ...
What aren't you seeing Mary?
[Silence]

Can you see what you are not seeing?
Yes.
What is it?
I see the where I I am it is the doctor. It is making me be ...
It is making you be what?
I can't be ... [unintelligible] ... later date.
Did you say that you would have it at a later date?
Yeah. [Sigh]
[Silence]

Are you ready to go to God?
I beg your pardon?
Are you ready to go to God?
No.

Do you think that being ready to go to God means that you are giving up?
[Silence]

You've got a frown on your face as if you are really thinking, but it doesn't seem to be able to come out. I don't think you are as well as you were last time I was here Mary!
Hey?
I can't get any kind of a conversation out of you.
[Silence]

If I pulled your nose, what would you do?
[Laugh]
I'm a naughty girl aren't I!
No you're not.

Does it feel better to be out of bed?
I'm not out.
Yes you are.
No I'm not.
You are in one of the lounging beds.
Oh.

What are you thinking Mary?
I'm sorry for you being so good.
Oh. Do you want me to be naughty?
[Silence]
You look a bit sad Mary. Are you feeling sad?
Not really.
What are you feeling?
[Silence for long period]

What are you thinking?
Things like they're all … [unintelligible] … what I have to do in then. I hope they need the next years I have to do …
I couldn't understand what you were saying because you were speaking very quietly. Could you say that again, Mary?
I don't know.

So, we are doing the book and we are doing the Introduction. The Introduction is about your illness and the last few years of your life. What

would you like to say to the people who are reading the book Mary?
Mm-hmm! I didn't know I was sick.
Well, dementia is a sickness.
Mm-hmm.
What do you think it is?
I didn't know what it was.
I would describe it as your brain not being well. Sickness is basically about something that doesn't work right. Dementia is about our brains not working right. It takes away our ability to communicate; takes away our ability to remember.
[Silence]

So what are you thinking?
About that.
What I just said?
What is going on.
Is that a question?
No.
You are thinking about what is going on?
Mm-hmm.
[Silence]

You still look a little sad!
You are or I am?
I think you are.
Very low.
You are very low—is that what you said?
Mm-hmm.
Why do you think you are very low?
I can't be what I've been.
You can't be what you have been? It happens when we get older - that we lose what we used to be.
[Silence]

So you are sad that you have lost so much because of the dementia? That you can't do the things that you used to do?
Mm-hmm.

31st January 2016

Thank you for coming to see me today. Where have you been?

I told Mary a little of what I had been doing for the past few hours.

I can't keep up with you.
You don't have too. Do you feel as if life is passing you by?
No! I'm thinking what the heck am I doing here.
In what sense?
No.

Interrupted by the nurses.

Are you feeling better than you did yesterday?
Yes, yes.
You slept better last night?
Yes.
Yesterday I could not get anything out of you. You were rather tired.

What are you thinking?
Did they let me come into the world?
Did who let you come into the world?
The world ... didn't we have a world when it started last week?
I do not know what you mean by the world Mary?
Oh. You don't know what the world is?

Well I do know that it is a big ball hanging around in space.
What was it?
My very energetic maid just swept up nine pins.
Hey?
Mercury, Venus, Earth, Mars, Jupiter, Saturn, Uranus, Neptune, Pluto—all part of our Solar System.
[Long silence]

I've been working on our book. I started writing the Introduction and I just thought—I should have asked this a long time ago! If someone was reading this book, what would you like to say to them in the Introduction?
You want me ...
To say something about what you would like said at the beginning of the book.
Um. um could I have it to has done what has been done. I'd like to read it.
Do you think that you could read it Mary?
Why?
I don't think you would understand a lot of it Mary because of the depth of your dementia. I am putting my foot further into my mouth here. It is over 170 pages long now and all it is about is our conversations.
Mm-hmm.

So, if you want to say anything to anybody about the book that we are writing what would you want to say?
It get to ... it doesn't worry me it doesn't get to me ...
[Silence]
So, you are not worried about the dementia?
Umm!
Do you want to talk about how hard a struggle it has been for you?
Yes.
What would you say about how it has been a hard struggle?
I don't what it something that sorry ...
You don't want people to be sorry for you?
No, no, no.
There is nothing to be sorry about?
Mm-hmm. You had a trickle about um dementia um on putting it aside blow them.
It's happened. That's life?
Yeah.

Do you think your faith has been affected in any way? Or has it made your faith stronger?

The dementia?

Yes!

Yes. Yes.

So you feel your faith is stronger because of the dementia?

[Silence]

I don't know how your faith could get any stronger because you are such a faith-filled woman. Your faith remains always strong, no matter what challenges life throws at you ... You want to hit me? You are frowning.

No. No I don't. I it did ahm ...

Disturbed by the nurse.

So we were talking about faith.

What did you say?

We were talking about faith.

[Silence]

I think if I was you I might say something like—my life has changed because of this illness. Initially I was angry about it. My faith has not changed. My faith remains strong even though I have this illness. Does that sound like you?

The other morning I got to one of the girls I said that I ahm she didn't say I said to myself I ahm at my head ahm I ahm yes tonight you've ... changing me.

What do you think 'at my head' means?

At my ...

'At my head' that is what you said.

What was at your head?

Yeah. I don't understand it. You said that.

[Silence]

No recollection?

No.

Do you think that you would ever read a book about someone going into dementia? Would you find that an interesting book?

No!

No. [Laugh]. Why are we writing this book then?

Why?

I don't know. There is something about this book that we are writing together ...

233

Yeah.

… I really had no reason. I was doing it because I thought that it was something that we could do together. And then the more that we got into the book or the more that we got into our conversations, um …

What's the book?

I am taping our conversations. That is what the book is about. Our conversations together. That is all it is about.

Mm-hmm.

The aim of the book I suppose is to show people how difficult it is for you to make conversation or to tell things; or remember things. To look at how that is happening over a period of time. Like yesterday, I could not get anything out of you.

What were you trying to get out of me?

I am not really trying to get anything out of you. I am just trying to see how well you are communicating. Can you understand this?

Ahm. I think there is something there but I'm um …

I suppose it is about what happens to a person's mind as their dementia gets worse. It takes away their ability to think properly and to function. And for you and me to have a conversation at any time, I have to start the conversations by asking you questions or telling you things that are going on—but mainly by asking you questions.

At the moment you have got your eyes closed. Some people might think that you are asleep but I know that you are awake and are listening to me because you have a frown on your forehead.

Oh! [Laugh] Do you that is fight and [garbled] …

I am not sure I understand what you are trying to say. In fact, I know I do not understand it. Sorry, Mary, that does not make sense to me.

Oh!

How do you feel when I say 'that doesn't make sense to me'? Is it frustrating that you can't make me understand what you are trying to say?

At the present um …

[Silence]

At the present what? It does frustrate you?

[Mary sighed]

Or are you just frustrated with this line of questioning?

No um I think it is just I … ah [sigh] … um ah …

Is your brain dribbling out your ears?

Yeah.

[Laughter]

You look really frustrated Mary.
Yes.
And why is that? Because you cannot understand?
No! [Emphatic] I'm … oh blow it!!!
No. Don't blow it. Try and get it out.
I can't do that.
Why?
Because you and other people help me to get it out.
I'd like to be able to help you get it out, but I cannot understand what you are trying to say. I think that you are frustrated that you cannot speak.
Yeah. Whatever it is that um comes from any of the works that um there is something that is lost …
Do you think part of Mary is lost?
Yes!
How does that make you feel?
It is love and abandoned too.
Love and abandoned, that is what you feel like?
Yeah.
You feel loved by somebody but you feel abandoned by somebody else?
Yes.
So, who do you feel abandoned by?
You.
Me.
No.
No?
No.
So who do you feel abandoned by Mary?
I don't think the people who once upon a would be
Do you feel abandoned by … ?
The sisters have not abandoned me but they do not know me anymore.
Do you know you anymore? Do you think anybody knows you anymore?
Yes I have to be Tully Morganed.
You have to be Tully Morganed?
Yeah. I have to I … I don't know what it is called.
Try and talk about it.
It's the garden that one in … doesn't come to me.
It doesn't come to you?
No. And there is no commitment but I just um … I am right out of um the place shot in my interest the mist come lost, lost, lost I had I can see all the people. Is there …

235

You can see that you are lost and you can see all the people there?
[Silence]
Or the people who have gone before you?
Yes.
Like your mother and father and Ilene?
Yes.
[Silence]

I have no inch of in my... [sigh]... I have no interest what I have back I have when I get that I think...

Mary started to cry.

I just don't know who I am.
You just don't know what?
I don't know who I am!
What I want?
It's I know what I want. I don't want anything!!!
I cannot understand why you are upset. I didn't hear it Mary. I really apologise. What made you cry?
There is nothing. That is why I am crying. I am so glad that you are there. I find it funny that I I my water runs down my eyes...

I wipe Mary's face.

Mary are you lonely?
I beg your pardon?
Are you lonely?
No I am not lonely. There is a very, very um... [mumble]... that's very ah I'm not it one time but there also... sigh... I'm so in the when I... [sigh]... there is not much interest in the my being the girl that was so the lady who was on the school last year um... I don't even know where they go now or...
[Silence]

What are you thinking?
I'm listening to a girl down the road.
[Silence]
Never get in.
The girl down the road never get in?
I was talking about a lady never they never lou out...
They never lou out?
Yeah. [Sigh!]

Why the big sigh?
I think ...
[Silence]

How do you feel when I tell you that you are deteriorating?
What's that say?
You are getting worse. How do you feel when I tell you that you are getting worse?
[Silence]
Does that scare you?
No.
Yeah.
I think anything that the only thing I have is love.
The only thing you have left is love?
Yes.
That is a powerful emotion to have left.
Yeah. Yeah.
Can you explain a bit what you mean by that?

When Mary is concentrating and seems to have difficulty in getting her words out, she starts to rapidly slap her hand against her body.

Left. Left. What is left is um me.
So what is left is love and what is left is me? Can you explain what you mean by that?
[Silence]

So you feel as if you've only got two things left–love and me.
Yes. What?
I was just thinking that you are an amazing lady.
[Laughter]
What is so funny about that?
[Laughter]
You don't feel amazing? Is that why you are laughing?
No.

They might send me to hospital.
You feeling unwell?
No. Shortly I will.
Shortly you will?
No, no, no, no. I'm not ... How have you done your work for today?

237

Hey?
When do you go down and back?
I leave in about 10 minutes actually.
Oh truly!
I will be back in a month. Can you last that long?
Yeah.
Good. I'd have to come and shoot you in the foot if you didn't.
[Laughter]

What are you thinking?
I am wondering if there is a woman who knows into the bubbly that you can get you know something that I can get down under that comes home into the yarn.
None of that makes any sense to me Mary.
Why?
I don't know.
[Laughter]
I am not on your wavelength sister.
[Long period of silence]

Oh dear I wish that I could stay.
What was that?
I'd love to stay.
[Silence]

Just know that I am always with you in spirit.
Yes
And if you need to go to the Lord before I come back, go to the Lord in peace.
Okay.
Don't struggle to stay in this life. You aren't struggling to stay alive are you Mary?
No.

[Sigh!]
That is a big sigh.
Yeah.
Why are you sighing?
I was just wondering who I ah you on the same track?
Am I on the same track? What track are you on?

Ahm. Jesus.
I don't think that you have lost your faith.
No! [Emphatic!]
Your path of prayer has taken a different track! You cannot do things like go on retreat. You don't get to mass. You have trouble saying or remembering to pray or meditate. But that doesn't stop you from being a woman of faith. You are just doing what you need to do.

Know that I am with you in spirit.
Thank you.

5th March 2016

I came into Mary's room to find that she was unconscious. Although she groaned at times, she did not speak to me again.

Thank you for walking with me on your journey Mary. Thank you for being my friend. Thank you for finding the beauty within me. Thank you for being my mate.

This is probably a little bit premature but ... 'May the blessing of God be upon you, the blessing of the Father and the Son, and may the spirit of God, the spirit of love be with you on your way.'

I'm going to miss you, your smile. I am going to miss making you laugh when I tell you stories. I am going to miss that really sharp wit of yours.

6th March 2016

I sit here and look at the face of my dying friend and know that we will not laugh together again; that we will not argue a point of order; we will not discuss an interesting subject; that we now walk the final physical path of our friendship.

I don't think that anybody ever feels that they have said goodbye well. I wished we had more time. I wish we had more to say, had more questions, more stories. Farewells are never perfect. This one wasn't either as I was interrupted by the arrival of some of the younger members of Mary's family.

I got to say goodbye. That is important. It is hard to believe that I will never see Mary alive again.

9th March 2016

Mary Magdalene Quinn took her final breath on the ninth day of March, 2016.

No more laughs or conversations together. They will forever remain only in my memory. I do know that she remembered those she loved most to the last. Towards the end, she might not have remembered names, but Mary's face would light with joy when one of her good friends walked into the room.

Mary spent her adult life serving the Lord in the best way she humanly could. She left this life with her faith undiminished.

Watching her deterioration over the last few years has been difficult, but I am grateful and honoured that Mary allowed me to share these years with her. To allow another to witness your vulnerability displays remarkable trust.

Living life will always be a struggle. Some of us will do it in relative comfort. Some will do it in abject misery. Whatever the journey, our final path that brings the last breath is something none can escape. For some it is a relief, for others a primal fear—but we all must face it. Some of us have paths that are relatively easy, while others suffer terribly. I know not the reason for this disparity, but what I have observed is the depth of character in those who have suffered; Those people have touched a level of their humanity that is a goal many of us strive for.

17th March 2016

Mary was buried yesterday. It hurts and I will miss her. I have lost the comfort of her friendship.

This was one of those times where the quiet reflection and celebration of a life past did not cut it for me. I think a bit of wailing with sackcloth and ashes would not have gone astray.

My grief vibrated through my body seeking relief from this full stop, this change in my friendship with my mate.

I sprinkled holy water onto her coffin. For me it symbolised the tears of God—appropriate I thought for someone who had served the Lord all her life.

I do not want to say farewell Mary, my friend, my mate, my teacher. But let you go?! Well, I have no choice. May the truth in your heart follow you through this next turning of your journey.

www.ingramcontent.com/pod-product-compliance
Lightning Source LLC
Chambersburg PA
CBHW031830090426
42741CB00005B/196